"*Smart Faith* will help you grow spiritually and live logically in an experience-driven culture. Read it if you're serious about your relationship with God!"

—STEVE RUSSO, international communicator; best-selling author;
cohost of *Life on the Edge Live!* radio show

"With razor-sharp clarity, Moreland and Matlock point out the serious lack of intellectual substance that characterizes the faith of most evangelicals. Readers will gain confidence for more effective evangelistic disciplemaking and be motivated to pursue the development of their minds for God's glory."

—JAY L. SEDWICK, PHD, associate professor of Christian education,
Dallas Theological Seminary

SMART FAI†H

LOVING YOUR GOD WITH ALL YOUR MIND

J.P. MORELAND & MARK MATLOCK

NAVPRESS ●

For a free catalog
of NavPress books & Bible studies call
1-800-366-7788 (USA) or 1-800-839-4769 (Canada).

www.NavPress.com

TH1NK
P.O. Box 35001
Colorado Springs, Colorado 80935

ISBN-13: 978-1-57683-734-4
ISBN-10: 1-57683-734-3

Cover design by Asterik Studio, Inc.
Creative Team: Gabe Filkey, Arvid Wallen, Laura Wright, Cara Iverson, Pat Reinheimer

The anecdotal illustrations in this book are composites of real situations, and any resemblance to people living or dead is coincidental.

Library of Congress Cataloging-in-Publication Data

Moreland, James Porter, 1948-
  Smart faith : loving your God with all your mind / J.P. Moreland and
Mark Matlock.
     p. cm.
  Includes bibliographical references.
  ISBN 1-57683-734-3
  1. Christian youth--Religious life. 2. Faith and reason. 3.
Apologetics. I. Matlock, Mark. II. Title.
  BV4531.3.M66 2005
  248.8'4--dc22

                          2005009693

Printed in the United States of America

4 5 6 7 8 9 10 / 11 10 09 08 07

CONTENTS

Good
Bad
Ugly

ACKNOWLEDGMENTS

I (J. P.) would like to acknowledge two groups of people who have helped make this book possible. First, the board of trustees and donors of Eidos Christian Center. Your support has been invaluable. Second, my church family at the Anaheim Vineyard, who combine the life of the mind with the power of the Spirit, especially Ken Slezak, Brian and Krista Slezak, Nigel Morris, Don Shortino, Lance Pittluck, Paul Frayla, and Dave and Geneva LeBates.

I (Mark) would like to acknowledge my church family at Irving Bible Church for continuing to love God with all their heart, mind, soul, and strength. Laura Wright provided amazing editorial assistance. Nicci Jordan, Terry Behimer, Gabe Filkey, Mike Kennedy, Cara Iverson, and everyone on "Th1nk Avenue" at NavPress that have a vision for creating high quality books for this generation, I applaud you all. Most of all, I thank my family, who lost me for a few weeks while I finished this book. Dad is done!

AUTHOR'S NOTE

Before you read this book, you should know a little bit about the people who wrote it and why they did. I'll start with J. P. Moreland, a philosopher and scholar who is the exact opposite of the personality type that just popped into your head. While J. P. is respected as a great Christian thinker, he is a real person. In fact, when we first visited about this book at his home in California, he made me a turkey sandwich, knowing I'd just come in from a long flight. In his sandals and untucked California beach shirt, he plopped on the sofa and told me about his wife and about his daughters, who were now out of college.

Having read several books and articles by J. P. (many of which were quite academic in nature), I knew that this man was capable of speaking way over my head, but he never did. What I saw was a man who had a wild passion for Jesus Christ that I imagine John the Baptist or Paul would have if they were living in our world today. J. P. is a real person who loves God not only with his mind but also with every part of himself. While we focus on the "mind" aspect in this book, please remember that we do because we feel it is the most neglected and misunderstood aspect of spiritual development in the church of America today. Our desire is that you would love God with your whole self and not just your intellect.

Now a little bit about me. I have worked with teenagers for

more than fifteen years. I produce and teach at weekend conferences called PlanetWisdom and work one-on-one with students through our website and in my local church. I have been married for twelve years and have two young children (right now they are six and eight). Although I am an ordained minister, I am not a scholar or an academic. In fact, a good chunk of my life and ministry has been as a professional magician (or illusionist)—something I seldom do anymore. As for school, I attended Biola University (where I first learned of J. P.) and left California to live in Texas in 1991. While I'm not what you would call the "best student," I have always believed that learning and good thinking are essential to being a disciple of Christ.

In working with students, I have found that many struggle in their life because they have not learned to develop an intellect that loves God. This generation needs this book, and I'm so thankful to have been a part of it.

Bottom line: J. P. and I are real people just like you. We aren't super-Christians or eggheads sitting in an office poring over textbooks. We want to love and serve God with every part of who we are. We wrote *Smart Faith* hoping it would help you discover this, too. Whether you are an intellectual giant or a person of average intelligence like myself, we all need to love God with our minds. I hope *Smart Faith* helps you to do just that.

Smart Faith may be one of the more challenging books you've chosen to read. While we've tried to make everything as easy to grasp as possible, there are some spots that may get a little thick. I want to encourage you to stick with it and move through the book to the end; you won't regret it, and the reward will be well worth it. As you seek to love God with all your mind, you will be shocked at how many new discoveries can be made as your relationship with the one true living God deepens. At the end of each chapter, we've included a section to help you go deeper into reflection about what it is you have read and how it applies to the real world you live in. You can read this book alone, but if you're like me, learning with others is much more fun. So buy a friend or two a copy (or make them buy their own!) and work through it together. May God lead you as you seek to increase your faith and to love God with all your mind.

Mark Matlock

Part I

GETTING SMART

HAVE WE LOST OUR MINDS?

FINDING COMPLETE FAITH

> *We live in what may be the most anti-intellectual period in the history of Western civilization. . . . We must have passion—indeed hearts on fire for the things of God. But that passion must resist with intensity the anti-intellectual spirit of the world.*
>
> R. C. Sproul

E-mail. We love it. We hate it. We love e-mail because it has increased the personal and meaningful contact that we can have with people. We hate it because we get way too much we don't want to respond to. That said, I (Mark) love getting e-mail from students. Many times I never know their names or where they are from. I'm sure that's the main reason they write me. They write with the hope that I have an answer to their questions or some advice to help them in their Christian walks. And they are brutally honest with me, I think, because they can remain anonymous. I don't know who they are, so they are guaranteed that any secrets are safe with me. Whether the writer is HugsforJesus or Coolio67, the names can't easily be traced back to an individual.

With all the secrecy you can bet there are lots of questions, both personal and troubling: about faith, relationships, sex, school, you name it. Who better to ask than someone who can't know who you are? Here's one from Randee regarding faith:

> I have a problem I don't feel I can share with anyone in my family or church. I'd like to think they might understand, but somehow I'm not so sure. Let me first tell you I was practically born in church; I can't ever remember a time when I didn't go. And when I say we go to church, I mean just about every time they will let us! Sunday, Wednesday, special events—our family is always there. So I've been a Christian all my life, and that is what my question is about.
>
> You see, I recently have become really good friends with someone who is a Hindu. I've been hanging out with the family, and while I don't necessarily think I believe anything they do, it got me to thinking. They were raised Hindu and believe with all their hearts that it's correct. I've been raised in a Christian home and church and have believed it, too. So is Jesus really the only way? Or do I believe that just because of the family I grew up with? I'm kind of doubting my faith right now and thinking that Christianity is just about as real as anything else out there, but it is such a pain in the neck to do the church thing if it really doesn't matter.

Have you ever felt the way Randee does? It's common when we are young to feel confident in our beliefs and yet at the same time be unable to explain why we believe. And when we can't explain, then it's just as easy to doubt. After all, if we don't have good answers for others, then why would we have good answers for ourselves?

THERE'S NO DOUBT WE'RE GOING TO DOUBT

Until the moment we have doubts, we may have received information about faith and accepted it without much question. But now that we're a little unsure, it's time to figure out how to own that faith for ourselves.

The good news is there's a reason we sometimes doubt our faith or are unable to defend it. This book will uncover and explore this reason—an underdeveloped intellect—and then offer a way to fix it. You see, to mature in our faith we need to develop our minds. This means studying the Bible as well as the world around us. Just one of the positive by-products of that lifetime effort will be having rational reasons for what we believe.

If you're thinking the explanation for lack in our faith seems simple while the solution seems a bit more challenging, you're right. But don't be scared away. Developing our minds will help us experience a complete *and* confident faith. This book will show us how.

"LOVE THE LORD YOUR GOD WITH ALL YOUR . . . MIND"

I've (Mark) received many e-mails like Randee's over the years. This doesn't make Randee's problem less important, but more. Experiences like hers help us recognize that an underdeveloped mind is a common issue many Christians face, especially (and ironically) those who have grown up in families focused on Christianity and church.

Unfortunately in our Christian culture today, much of our spiritual growth tends to be in the areas of emotion and sheer tenacity. There is nothing wrong, of course, with having strong emotions toward God, experiencing His presence in our worship, or clinging to the belief that Jesus is the way. In fact, these are all appropriate aspects of Christianity. But without a healthy intellect, these areas fall out of balance. We become less than God asks us to be in our Christian walk. Sometimes we even lose faith completely.

How have we come to this conclusion? Well, when Jesus was questioned about which commandment was the greatest, He responded, "Love the Lord your God with all your heart and with all your soul and with all your strength and with all your mind" (Luke 10:27). Jesus is saying here that He wants us to love God with the *total* person that we are. If we can offer only emotional arguments for our faith and not solid intellectual ones, then we're in trouble.

Believers have not always suffered from this problem, so we're going to take a brief look back to how we got into this situation. Then we'll have the right first-aid supplies to put our minds back in proper working order.

As you read, remember that on the journey toward a well-rounded faith, you don't have to be embarrassed about doubting or asking questions. Most Christians have gone through times when they have big questions about their faith in Jesus Christ. That's normal. Asking honest questions is often the straightest path to finding answers.

WHERE'S OUR SALT?
INTELLECTUALISM TAKES A BLOW

Seventh grade was a breakthrough year for me (Mark). While I was attending a public junior high school, my history teacher spent an entire week paralleling the development of the Middle East, Christianity, Islam, and the Bible. For the first time, the study of history made sense to me, and because the teacher was a believer, he integrated his study with historical accounts from the Bible. I was fascinated.

As I began the pursuit of developing wisdom in my life, I realized that history was a great teacher. As the saying goes, "Smart people learn from their own mistakes; wise people learn from others' mistakes." But history also helps us understand who we are. Knowing things about our past can help us understand why we are who we are today. So let's take a brief look at how the minds of past believers were involved in their faith.

While generalizations can be misleading, it is safe to say that from the arrival of the Pilgrims to the middle of the nineteenth century, American believers prized the intellectual life for its contribution to the Christian journey. Christian values were woven into private *and* public life. Remember the Puritans? While they are often portrayed as fundamentalist, close-minded individuals responsible for the Salem witch trials, they were incredible people, and we actually owe much of our quality of life to them.

The Puritans' desire was to purify the church of England and place it under the authority of Scripture rather than the authority of the king or the pope. Some Puritan groups were called "separatists" and were persecuted for their beliefs. In 1620, roughly 100 passengers on the Mayflower made the trip to America. They arrived on the shores of Massachusetts, forming their own government based on a document called the Mayflower Compact, which was signed by forty-one of the passengers, thirty-seven of which were persecuted Puritans. Ten years later, some fifty-five thousand English colonists came to Massachusetts. One of their leaders was John Winthrop, who envisioned them creating a "city upon a hill"—an example for all the nations of how godly people live.

Puritans were highly educated people. In an agricultural economy in which academic pursuits were usually not essential for those who worked the land, Puritans founded colleges (yes, they started Harvard; when it opened, bears would often run through the campus as classes were conducted!); taught their children to read and write before the age of six; and studied art, science, and philosophy as a way of loving God with their minds. Ministers were seen as not only spiritual authorities but also intellectual authorities in their communities.[1] Scholars such as Jonathan Edwards were activists who desired to be knowledgeable in spiritual matters as well as a variety of other disciplines. Cotton Mather, a well-known Puritan, proclaimed, "Ignorance is the Mother not of Devotion but of HERESY."[2]

What happened so that intellectualism and Christianity went down different roads? In the 1700s and 1800s, dramatic events took place that wrestled intellectualism out of the arms of the church.

"GREAT" AWAKENINGS

The seeds for a shift away from the Christian mind were planted in the United States during what is called the First Great Awakening. What appeared to be a great time of revival for the church can now be considered the beginning of intellectual demise. The preaching of a man named George Whitefield in the mid-1700s was characterized by a new kind of preaching: It was popular, stylized, and emotional. In the first half of the 1800s, three more similar awakenings followed in which "anti-intellectualism was a feature."[3]

While many results of these movements were positive, their overall effect was negative to Christianity in America. For example, the movements emphasized immediate personal conversion to Christ instead of a studied period of reflection and conviction before conversion. Emotionally charged, simple messages—rather than intellectually careful and doctrinally precise sermons—became the norm. Personal feelings, along with an emphasis on a right relationship with Christ, became the most important feature of conversion. This was in place of a deep grasp of the nature of Christian teaching and ideas.

This doesn't sound all bad, does it? That might be because these shifts describe our church communities today, and we're accustomed to thinking these are the best ways to encourage people to convert.

We think it works—until we find ourselves as believers unable to identify what or why exactly we believe.

Really, nothing is wrong with presenting Christ to the masses by focusing on personal conversion, as was the new method during these revivals. Many people begin their walk with Christ amid highly emotional circumstances in which Christ is offered as a practical solution to their problems. Feelings are important. Knowing that Christ will meet needs is important. But emotion and inward-focused concerns aren't enough to *sustain* people in their Christian walk. Think of the seed falling on shallow soil in Matthew 13:

> "A farmer went out to sow his seed. As he was scattering
> the seed, some fell . . . on rocky places, where it did not have
> much soil. It sprang up quickly, because the soil was shallow.
> . . . The one who received the seed that fell on rocky places
> is the man who hears the word and at once receives it with
> joy. But since he has no root, he lasts only a short time.
> When trouble or persecution comes because of the word, he
> quickly falls away." (verses 3-5,20-21)

If we find ourselves in trouble the minute someone (including our own thoughts) challenges us from a factual, historical, or intellectual point of view, then we need some intellectual backup. We need heart *and* head belief.

But unfortunately, partly because of this history, today we must overcome an intellectually shallow, theologically illiterate form of Christianity.

CULTS FILL AN INTELLECTUAL VACUUM

Another negative result—and a tragic one at that—was the number of cults that rose up and took advantage of the lack of Christian foundation in many new converts. Mormonism, Jehovah's Witnesses, and Christian Science arose in the 1800s, often finding success in areas after Christian revivals left unstable and untaught converts open to theological deception. Cotton Mather's warning about ignorance leading to heresy was clearly disregarded during this era.

UNPREPARED FOR BOLD NEW PHILOSOPHY

The anti-intellectual emphasis in the church then created a lack of readiness for the full-on intellectual battle Christianity would face in the late 1800s. New ideas from Europe, led by philosophers such as David Hume and Immanuel Kant, altered people's understanding of religion. While many of these ideas are widely accepted today and surround us in society, these ideas were revolutionary in their day.

Hume claimed that the traditional arguments for God's existence (for example, the world is an effect that needs a personal cause) were quite weak. He also said that because we cannot experience God with the five senses, the claim that God exists cannot be taken as an item of knowledge. For slightly different reasons, Kant came to the same conclusion. Kant asserted (in a similar way) that human knowledge is limited to what can be experienced with the five senses, and because God cannot be so experienced, we cannot know God exists. The shared viewpoint of these two great thinkers was like a one-two punch at the case for God.

As these philosophies spread and grew popular, confidence was lost in the existence of God and the rationality of the Christian faith. How can faith be reasonable if it can't be verified with the five senses? Fewer and fewer people regarded the Bible as a body of divinely revealed, true propositions about various topics that require devoted study to grasp. Instead the Bible became viewed as merely a source of ethical guidance and spiritual growth.

CRITICISM CHALLENGES THE HISTORICAL ACCURACY OF THE BIBLE

At this same time, German criticism challenged the historical accuracy of the Bible. Authorship of books of the Bible was questioned, and a search for the historical Jesus was launched.

Unable to adequately defend against the criticisms that arose, Christians actually became less inclined to study the historical context of Scripture. People began to see Scripture reading as personal and so "devotionalized" it, considering it an opportunity for personal experience rather than understanding it in its literary and historical contexts. It came to be believed that only the Holy Spirit was needed to experience the truth of Scripture while no intellectual exercise was needed for spiritual growth.

DARWINISM CHALLENGES CREATIONISM

These cultural conditions made fertile ground for Darwin's theory of evolution to become popular. Darwinian evolution challenged the place of God in the creation of the world, the historical accuracy of Genesis, and the existence of God entirely.[4] The theory offered a safe harbor for those who rejected creationism and even God. Our society of faith was being replaced with the secular society we have today.

LOSING OUR SALT

Jesus said, "You are the salt of the earth. But if the salt loses its saltiness, how can it be made salty again?" (Matthew 5:13). Instead of responding to these attacks on Christianity with a salty counterpunch, many believers grew suspicious of intellectual issues altogether. After all, who wants to fight battles that end in loss and shame? Of course we need to rely on the help of the Holy Spirit in our intellectual pursuits, but this doesn't mean we can avoid the often-difficult task of thinking intelligently when defending our faith.

Around the turn of the nineteenth century, fundamentalists withdrew from the broader intellectual culture and from the war with liberals (there was a culture war then, too!) and focused inward. They established their own Bible institutes and concentrated on lay-oriented Bible and prophecy conferences. This withdrawal from intellectual and public life contributed to the isolation of the church, the reduction of Christian ideas in public arenas, and the shallowness and trivialization of Christian living, thought, and activism.

In short, the culture lost its salt. And this describes the situation today. We now live in a Christian culture so deeply committed to a nonintellectual way of understanding Christian faith that this perspective is now imbedded within us at a subconscious level. You didn't misread. Our underlying ideas about Christianity affect how we think church should be, what a good sermon is, what is worth giving our money to, how we should raise our families, where we go to college, what we should study, and a host of other topics in our lives.

But if our faith is central to how we live and what we believe is flawed, then how we live out our Christianity will be filled with flaws as well. Our modern understanding of Christianity in this area is inconsistent with the Bible and with most of Christian history. If you aren't yet convinced, consider the following impacts of a weakened Christian mind. They will probably sound familiar.

Blind Faith

Faith is now understood as a blind act of will—a decision to believe something independent of reason or as a simple choice while ignoring the lack of evidence for what is believed. In contrast, biblical faith is a power or skill to act in accordance with the nature of the kingdom of God, a trust in what we have reason to believe is true. This is faith built on reason.

A faith without reason may be the source of Randee's dilemma.

From her e-mail we can infer that she has been merely socialized into Christianity: She goes to church not because she has a strong reason to but because that's what she's been taught to do. Randee hasn't been discipled into a deep, sure faith.

Randee is certainly not alone. Research from The Barna Group, a company devoted to collecting and evaluating religious trends, reports that 58 percent of all active church-attending teenagers won't be attending church by their thirtieth birthday![5] It wouldn't be a stretch to believe that this is because the faith they acquired early on didn't take root. Likely they were missing the intellectual aspects of faith.

The Separation of Church and . . . Everything

Christian teaching and practice are private and separate from public or so-called secular activities. Religion has thus become personal, private, and too often simply a matter of how we feel about things. In contrast, the culture encourages us to invoke our intellect in secular, public life, but not in faith matters. (Think about how we're encouraged to use our intellect in how we approach what college we'll go to, what car we'll buy, and so on.)

When Christians withdrew from public discourse, they took the Christian worldview with them. One of the results is that three of the major centers of influence in our culture—universities, media, and government—are typically missing a spiritual perspective to life. And even as believers, we are missing this perspective as well when our faith has little impact on parts of our lives besides church (such as what major we choose and whether we impact for Christ those in our classes). (We will help you integrate your faith into your whole life later in this book.)

The Christian worldview was once the foundation to every aspect of culture, but it is now rarely invited to participate. And when we do contribute on certain topics, we either struggle to explain faith intelligently or we are mocked out of the arena.

Twisting the Good News

World missions are weakened. Just as cults followed the theologically lacking revivals of the past, today it is common for misunderstanding and incorrect theology to follow the efforts of missions. In one example, a Christian leader from Central America exhorted North American mission agencies to stop sending evangelists to his country because their efforts were producing Marxists bent on overthrowing the government. This was because there were "Christian" thinkers in his country that held to liberation theology, a form of Marxism draped in religious garb. These "Christians" were attracting the thinking leaders among the converts and training them in Marxist ideology, which the liberals identified as the true center of biblical theology!

Making the Gospel Irrelevant

We offer an irrelevant gospel. As we've mentioned, today we share the gospel primarily as a means of addressing felt needs. We give testimonies of our changed life and tell people that Christ is the answer to troubles. As true and powerful as these may be, this approach ultimately doesn't cut it for two reasons: (1) it doesn't reach people who may be out of touch with their feelings, and (2) it invites the response, "Sorry, but I don't have a need. I'm doing just fine with my life."

Shamed into Silence

We suffer from a loss of boldness in confronting ideas in our culture with an effective Christian witness. We've touched on this earlier, but in addition, for those who lack courage, anti-intellectualism has created a context in which we often come off as shallow, defensive, and reactionary instead of thoughtful, confident, and articulate.

At school, at work, and sometimes at home, even identifying yourself as a Christian is often considered the same as wearing a sign that says, "Village Idiot." The way intellectuals in our country react to our claims of faith is enough to send us running for cover in shame. But if we develop our minds, we'll find ourselves boldly and intelligently taking on the challenge.

MINISTERING TO A SECULAR CULTURE

Our culture today is primarily secular, and the primary issue today is knowledge. Knowledge is power. (Think about all the people who use the Internet to acquire health information and make decisions on doctors and treatments, as just one example!) For many secularists, knowledge is obtained solely by means of the senses and science (remember Hume and Kant?). Today, knowledge is identical to *scientific* knowledge. Science supposedly deals with facts, truths, and reason, but religion and ethics supposedly deal with subjective private opinions. (By the way, J. P. and I aren't against science, but we do reject the idea that science and science alone can give us knowledge.)

Secular views of knowledge have replaced Christian ideals of knowledge because religion and ethics are neither scientifically testable nor compatible with evolution. A secular worldview is responsible for the following social trends. Knowing about these, recognizing them, and learning to effectively combat them (we will show you how in this book) will help make you a potent player in God's kingdom.

- Traditional interpretations of morality (based on biblical guidelines and nature) are considered passé. Today's translation: Morality is relative.
- The definition of *the good life* has changed. From Old Testament times until this century, the good life was understood to mean a life of intellectual and moral virtue. Happiness was understood as a life of virtue, and

the successful person was one who knew how to live life well according to the creative design of God. Today's translation: The good life means material success and public notoriety.

- Freedom was traditionally understood as the power to do what one ought to do. And *individual rights* were important, but virtue and duty were more central than rights. Today's translation: Freedom means we look out for number one.

- *Tolerance* of the views of others meant that even though we might think those views wrong and will argue against them, we will defend the rights of others to argue their cases. We will also treat the other with respect as an image bearer of God. Today's translation: Tolerance means we must shut up if we don't agree.

WHAT CAN WE DO?

Don't let this information or Satan's schemes bring you down. God wants to use you. So allow this to motivate you to read on—to discover how finding your mind and loving God with it will inspire your spiritual journey.

Recent signs of our culture paying more attention to Christians and the potential power they wield are encouraging. And you have a chance to be part of that influence by making sure you seek excellence in developing your mind so that you can become a powerful leader for Christ in whatever arena you inhabit. The rest of this book will help you do that.

SMART THINKING

Consider now what type of question-and-answer person you are. Do any of the following describe you or the people around you?

- *Question Avoiders* want to hide their lack of knowledge, so they try to make others feel foolish for asking questions.
- *Simple-Answer People* offer "bumper sticker" answers that may be true but don't really help, such as "The Bible says so" or "Let go and let God."
- *Question Lovers* appear to be honestly pursuing truth, but in reality they love questions more than finding answers.
- *Truth Seekers* realize they don't know everything (a good sign they may actually know something) and will join you in your struggle to find answers.

Isn't it obvious? We want you to be counted as a Truth Seeker. Your spiritual growth will come easier that way, so ask God to help you get an honest picture of yourself. If you're not quite a genuine Truth Seeker, what will you do to change that?

CHAPTER TWO

HOW OUR MINDS MAP FAITH

THINKING WILL TAKE US FAR

*The scandal of the evangelical mind is that there is not much of
an evangelical mind. . . . Despite dynamic success at a popular
level, modern American evangelicals have failed notably
in sustaining serious intellectual life. They have nourished
millions of believers in the simple verities of the gospel but
have largely abandoned the universities, the arts, and other
realms of "high" culture. . . . The historical situation is . . .
curious. Modern evangelicals are the spiritual descendants of
leaders and movements distinguished by probing, creative,
fruitful attention to the mind.*

MARK NOLL

At a summer party with my youth group, I (Mark) stood on
the edge of the swimming pool and prayed, *I believe.* I stepped
out hoping to walk on the water just as Jesus and Peter did, but I sank.
Hovering near the bottom of the pool, I wondered if God was real.
I was frustrated. Didn't the Bible teach that only faith as small as a
mustard seed was needed to move mountains? *Surely then,* I thought,
I have enough faith to walk on water.

I lay in bed that night wondering what I needed to do to have
more faith. I came to the conclusion that I would have to be willing to

put my life on the line. With my life at stake, all my faith would have to be strong or else I would die. Tomorrow, I decided, I would try to fly—using my faith in God.

School got out early because of a pep rally. I hurried home to test my faith. Out on the lawn I thought through my plan. I would run as hard as I could and then jump with all my strength into the air. My faith would keep me from falling. I started to run and then stopped. Jumping into the air over grass (and a mattress I brought outside) didn't really require much faith. Jumping over cement would be much more dangerous and would require more faith.

So I went to stand by the street. I waited for the cars to pass and then walked out to the broken yellow line. In my mind I said, *Run as fast as you can and then jump into the air. Your faith in God will keep you from falling.* I got ready to run and then stopped. What if I ran and jumped and I did fall? I might lose some skin, spill some blood, and crack a rib or two—but I wouldn't die. So I decided that in order to really prove I had faith in God to save me, I would have to jump off the roof of my two-story house. I ran and climbed out onto the roof. As I peered over the edge to the driveway fifty feet below, I realized that if I ran and jumped I would surely die, unless God was really real and He saved me.

Now, what do you think happened when I jumped? You'll never really know, because I decided against the idea. Did I really lack faith in God? Nope, not one bit. What I did come to realize was how poor my understanding of faith was. My idea was that if I believed really hard in God, I could fly. But this was not reasonable. Hebrews 11:1 teaches us that "faith is the substance of things hoped for, the evidence of things not seen" (KJV). Faith is not wishful thinking; faith is a reasoned confidence. Standing on the roof, I had no reason to have faith that God would not let me fall.

WHY IS REASON IMPORTANT TO OUR FAITH?

As we revealed in chapter 1, the faith we talk about most often in church is understood as a blind act of the will, a decision to believe something independent of reason or as a simple choice while ignoring the lack of evidence for what is believed. We're not suggesting you've never thought of reasons for your faith (though we might challenge you to produce them in a brief but coherent manner right this minute), but we are saying that how the mind works in our spirituality is more than just a list of reasons to believe. It's a whole way of being. This chapter will look at what faith really is and how our minds must be involved to make us whole and balanced Christians.

We'll be using the word *reason* often in this book, so it is important that we give you a definition. Reason is not something that we see as being in opposition to faith or revelation. Instead, it is all the abilities we have that can be used to gain knowledge and justify our beliefs about different issues. For example:

- Through our senses, we can see, hear, smell, taste, and feel. At the zoo, we can observe that an animal is big, gray, and rough-skinned.
- Through memory we can remember what has already occurred (the past). By recalling the past, we can remember that some huge, gray, rough-textured animals are called elephants. We can also recall other information about them that we may have learned (even without having seen a real one), such as their habitat.
- Through my abilities of logic, I know that some whales are huge and gray and have rough skin but that they also live in large bodies of water and do not have legs. So I can conclude that this is an elephant.

■ Through my moral faculties, I know that caring for sick
elephants is kind and that killing them just for their ivory
tusks is wrong.

So by reason, we are talking about the use of these abilities either
alone or combined to gain knowledge and justify our beliefs.

GOD IS REASONABLE

God is a God of reason. We know this because of the character and
actions of God described in the Bible. The Bible teaches, for example,
that God's unique attributes include omniscience: He is perfect in
knowledge and knows everything (see 1 Samuel 23:11-13; Job 37:16;
1 John 3:20). The Bible also describes Him as the only "wise God"
(Romans 16:27), the God of truth who cannot lie (see Titus 1:2), and
completely reliable (see Romans 3:4; Hebrews 6:18). God's very Word
is true (see John 17:17), and His church — not the university — is the
pillar and support of the truth (see 1 Timothy 3:15). Most amazing
of all, the God of the Bible invites His creatures to come and reason
with Him (see Isaiah 1:18) by bringing a legally reasoned case against
His actions to which He will respond (see Ecclesiastes 6:10; Jeremiah
12:1; 20:12).

Compare this portrait of God with what we know of other gods.
With Islam, we have a god who is so transcendent that he is beyond
understanding. The Greek gods and the gods of other polytheistic
(having many gods) religions such as Hinduism are fickle, are swayed
by their emotions, and act inconsistently. The God of the Bible never
changes (see James 1:17), requires teachers who diligently study His
Word and handle it accurately (see 1 Timothy 4:15-16; 2 Timothy
2:15), and requires His evangelists to be able to give a rational justification for what they believe to all who ask (see 1 Peter 3:15).

With the monistic (reality consisting of a single element)

religions of the East, we are offered meditations—like the sound of one hand clapping—to escape logical thought. (If you think about one hand clapping too long, you'll lose your mind!) The Buddhist is to leave her mind behind, but God asks the Christian to be transformed by the renewing of her mind (see Romans 12:1-2).

No wonder Christians started the first universities and have planted schools and colleges everywhere missionaries have gone. No wonder science began in Christian Europe—after all, the same rational God who made the rational human mind also created the rational world so the mind would be suited to figure out the world's structure.

God created you to be a follower of Christ with your mind turned on and tuned in to the life He made for you. This does not mean God loves scholars and academics more than He loves other people. (Look at all the types of folks Jesus hung out with and counted as His own!) But if virtues mirror our God of perfection, then ignorance is not a Christian virtue.

GOD'S REVELATION POINTS TOWARD REASON

God is also a God of revelation. God reveals Himself to us in many ways. He reveals Himself through creation. This revelation is so powerful that humans have no excuse for not knowing by it who He is (see Romans 1:20). He reveals Himself through His Son, who lived among us and became a human participant in history. And He reveals Himself through His Word. These revelations point us toward the importance of developing our Christian mind.

Truth Is Available

The Bible as revelation from God has great implications for our Christian minds. The central biblical terms for *revelation* are *galah*[6] (Hebrew) and *apocalupto* and *phaneroo* (Greek). These words express the idea of revealing, disclosing, and making known. When we say that the Bible is revelation from God, we mean that He can be known through it. But we also mean that God has revealed understandable, objectively true ideas. So God's Word is not only useful but also theoretically true (see John 17:17).

God has revealed Himself to us, and He has revealed truth itself to us. He gives this truth to our minds with the intention that we use our intellects to understand truth and apply it to our lives.

The Holy Spirit Provides Inspiration and Application

Maybe you are wondering how the Holy Spirit is involved. The Bible does contain portions that are easily grasped, but as you know, because of the Bible's nature, serious study is needed to grasp all that it says. In fact, Peter once said that some of Paul's writings were intellectually challenging, hard to understand, and easily distorted by those untrained in Christian theology (see 2 Peter 3:16). If you have ever tried to understand the depths of Romans or Ephesians, you know what Peter was talking about!

Hermeneutics is the science of interpreting, and the more you understand of this, the more Scripture will mean to you. Unfortunately, many people do not want to learn the hard way (incidentally, there is no easy way!); they want to believe that the Holy Spirit will help them understand the meaning of everything they read. This is a common misunderstanding of the role of the Holy Spirit. His job is really to speak to our souls, convicting, comforting, and showing us applications of biblical truth. To follow are two passages people typically use to claim that the Holy Spirit will make everything clear.

> But the Helper, the Holy Spirit, whom the Father will send in My name, He will teach you all things, and bring to your remembrance all that I said to you. (John 14:26, NASB)

A simple reading of this passage makes it easy to assume that our common idea about the Holy Spirit is true. But a more careful reading of the passage reveals that no promise is made that the Holy Spirit will teach the meaning of Scripture to believers. Instead, the passage promises the apostles that the Spirit will inspire them and aid them in remembering the words of Jesus. The verse is spoken specifically to the disciples and not to believers in general. Several other passages (see John 14:1,25,28-29; 16:16; 17:12-14,26) support this as well.

> You have no need for anyone to teach you; but as His
> anointing teaches you about all things, and is true and is not
> a lie, and just as it has taught you, you abide in Him. (1 John
> 2:27, NASB)

Some people take this passage to mean that the Holy Spirit teaches the believer and that there is no need for a teacher to understand the Bible—no need for Sunday school, Bible studies, commentaries, or seminaries. Common sense tells us this cannot be true. Read the 1 John passage again. If we apply our thinking skills, it seems obvious. If John is telling us we don't need a teacher, then we wouldn't need John to tell us that we don't need a teacher! On top of that, the New Testament provides multiple examples of gifted teachers—given by God to His people—who are diligent in their teaching (see Ephesians 4:11). It is God's intention for us to use our minds and reason when we approach His Word. Part of that responsibility is to make sure we study Scripture in context.

When cultists come to my (J. P.'s) door, I often point out that they take passages out of context. To prove this, I ask them to name the historical setting, main theme, and basic structure of just one of the sixty-six books of the Bible. If someone is in the habit of studying Scripture properly and with an eye on context, he or she should have the ability to do this. I have never once had a cultist accept my challenge.

Scripture Commands the Development of Our Minds

So we know that the Bible offers truth and the Holy Spirit helps us apply it. Now we just have to study it. Says who? God does, through three important Scriptures that command the development of our minds.

> I urge you, brethren, by the mercies of God, to present
> your bodies a living and holy sacrifice, acceptable to God,
> which is your spiritual service of worship. And do not
> be conformed to this world, but be transformed by the
> renewing of your mind, that you may prove what the will
> of God is, that which is good and acceptable and perfect.
> (Romans 12:1-2, NASB)

These words are no doubt familiar to you, but the critical point Paul makes is that we cannot prove (make known to ourselves and others) what God's will is without the renewing or transformation of our minds. So here we are with our minds front and center to our spiritual development! We all want to know God's will, and this text is telling us we can't know it unless we present our bodies (including our souls and minds) to the Lord for transformation and renewal.

When an expert in Mosaic Law challenged Jesus to summarize the entire Old Testament, this was how Jesus replied:

> "'Love the Lord your God with all your heart and with
> all your soul and with all your mind.' This is the first and
> greatest commandment. . . . And the second is like it: 'Love
> your neighbor as yourself.'" (Matthew 22:37-39)

The idea is very clear that we are to love God with every part of our being, including the intellectual one: our mind. Even though Jesus was God, He was also human, and during most of His earthly life, He subordinated His divine nature to His Father and lived as a regular human being. The Bible tells us that He grew in knowledge, learned things, and so on. We are to do the same.

What would it look like for the church, a parent, or you to try to nurture an intellectual love of God? Just before His answer to the Sadducees' question, Jesus Himself gives us a hint of what it might mean to love God with our minds. In Matthew 22:22-23, a group of Sadducees who did not believe in the resurrection of the dead tried to trap Jesus with an intellectual argument involving a story of a woman who had been married to seven brothers, one right after the other. The Sadducees asked Jesus whose wife the woman would be in the Resurrection. Jesus' options for response seemed to be (1) deny the Resurrection, (2) accept polygamy and adultery by affirming her marriage to all seven in heaven, or (3) unfairly and arbitrarily limit her marriage to one brother only. Not very good options!

Well, I'm sure you can guess what Jesus did. He *intellectually* responded to the Sadducees' question. First He denied the condition for the Sadducees' argument to even get started; that is, He said there was no marriage in heaven. Then Jesus addressed the deeper issue about the Resurrection. He quoted a verse that, on the surface, appears not to be related particularly to the issue of the Resurrection: "'I AM THE GOD OF ABRAHAM, AND THE GOD OF ISAAC, AND THE GOD OF JACOB.' He is not the God of the dead but of the living" (Matthew 22:32, NASB). Wouldn't a verse such as Daniel 12:2 be more effective since it specifically affirms the Resurrection? No, because Jesus knew by studying Sadducean theology that they did not fully accept the authority of the prophets, including Daniel. Jesus also knew that the passage He did use was a critical verse for the Sadducees. So Jesus' argument hinged on the tense of the verb. He did not say, "I *was* the God of Abraham" but "I *am* . . ." This claim could be true only if Abraham and the others continued to exist.

Jesus revealed His intellectual skills in this debate by (1) showing His familiarity with His opponents' points of view, (2) appealing to common ground (Scripture that all accepted), and (3) using the laws of logic to refute His opponents' arguments. Because the debate comes immediately before Matthew 22:37-39, it may tell us at least in part what it means to love God intellectually: *Be prepared to stand up for God's truth and honor when they are challenged, and do so with carefully thought-out answers.*

> AND DO NOT FEAR THEIR INTIMIDATION, AND DO NOT BE TROUBLED, but sanctify Christ as Lord in your hearts, always being ready to make a defense *[apologia]* to everyone who asks you to give an account *[logos]* for the hope that is in you, yet with gentleness and reverence. (1 Peter 3:14-15, NASB)

Peter makes two key points with these verses. The first is that we need to be able to defend *(apologia)* what we believe. We need to make positive arguments for what we believe as well as defend against negative attacks, just as one would in a courtroom. The apostle Paul did this often in evangelism (see Acts 14:15-17; 17:2,4,17-31; 18:4; 19:8). He persuaded people to become Christians by offering rational arguments for the truth of the gospel. He even cited nonbelieving poets and philosophers as part of his case! Could you do this right now in your life? Peter was not just *suggesting* we do this; he was *commanding* believers to be ready.

The second point Peter makes is that we must be able to offer evidence or argument that provides rational justification for a belief *(logos)*. We must have true belief plus evidence to back up that belief. While you're gathering your evidence, just be sure to remember Peter's reference to gentleness, which implies we are to argue but not be argumentative.

Now let's take a moment and remember who is writing this to us: Peter, the fisherman! You might expect to hear this from Paul or from a professor of biblical studies, but Peter was uneducated. Compare the Peter of the Gospels with the Peter who makes his first sermon in Acts. An amazing transformation. He had learned so much in following Christ, and then he was inspired and aided by the Holy Spirit in his message. When we consider Peter's story in the Bible, we see him developing his mind and reasoning abilities throughout his life — exactly the point of this book.

Knowledge Is Available Outside the Bible

Scripture, especially the accounts of the life of Christ, is a unique and reliable source for understanding truths God has revealed to us. Holy Scripture is the central object of study in loving God with the mind. But Scripture also shows us the value of extrabiblical knowledge for (1) developing a life of wisdom, (2) knowing the value of natural moral law, and (3) ultimately ministering from a position of influence.

Developing a Life of Wisdom. The Bible has a lot to say about reverence for God as wisdom (see Proverbs 1:7), but such reverence alone doesn't bring wisdom. Wisdom results when a respectful heart is united with a disciplined mind. We get knowledge from study, and knowledge is necessary for wisdom. God reveals Himself and truth through common sense, logic, and mathematics, along with the arts, humanities, sciences, and other areas of study — all of which contain important truths about life.

According to the Bible, wisdom comes from studying nature as well as learning Scriptures. One such passage instructs the lazy person to observe the ants — to consider their ways and be wise (see Proverbs 6:6). Scripture also acknowledges the wisdom of cultures outside Israel (see Isaiah 19:11-13; Jeremiah 49:7; Zechariah 9:2).

Knowing the Value of Natural Moral Law. The Bible repeatedly acknowledges the existence of true moral principles rooted in the way God made things knowable to all people independent of the Bible (see Job 31:13-15; Romans 1 and 2). It is this natural and moral law that allows people who do not study Scripture to know morality apart from Christ. This also means believers do not always have to appeal to Scripture when arguing certain moral positions, such as homosexual marriage and abortion. For example, if you examine a car key, you can see that it was designed to fit into the ignition and not, say, into a basketball hoop! Similarly, observation of male and female body parts make it obvious that they were designed to fit together and that, say, a male's body was not designed to fit another male.

Because moral law is around us and in us, Christians should work to form a moral and just government, not a theocracy. The government should not be placed under Scripture. The necessary guidance for justice of Romans 13:1-7 is found in natural moral law — enough for the government to do its job. Of course Christians are to *preach* to unbelievers what Scripture says about some topic, but when believers argue for or defend their views in the public arena with those who do not accept Scripture, they should use general principles of moral argument and reasoning.

The prophet Amos did just this. He denounced the moral behavior of several nations outside of Israel and never once appealed to Scripture for his arguments. Natural moral law, which he assumed was known by those without Scripture, was suitable for him to argue his case. Only when he rebuked Israel did he bring out "the law of the LORD" (Amos 2:4). Amos appealed to the common ground, just as Jesus did with the Sadducees (see Matthew 22:23-33) and as Paul did when evangelizing the Greeks (see Acts 17:16-31).

Ministering from a Position of Influence. Excelling at an understanding of extrabiblical (in addition to biblical) knowledge fortifies us with influence. Consider Daniel and his friends who were taken captive by King Nebuchadnezzar to serve in his courts. God put them in position to minister to the king of Babylon in His name because they showed "intelligence in every branch of wisdom" (Daniel 1:3-4, NASB; see 2:12-13; 5:7). These men had worked hard to learn Babylonian science, geometry, and literature, and because of this, they were prepared to serve when the occasion presented itself.

Unfortunately, this is not the case in our country. There are few Christians leading in key areas of influence in our nation because there are simply not enough believers with the intellectual and professional excellence necessary. Condoleezza Rice, our secretary of state, is a wonderful exception who stands as an encouragement and challenge to all Christians.

Will the next generation impact this situation for the better? According to various studies, increasing numbers of college freshmen say their primary goal in going to college is to get a good job and ensure a secure financial future. These same students also value a good job more than developing a meaningful philosophy of life. Do you fit into this category? We know it's easy to lose sight of what God wants for us. That's why we want you to use this book to identify, challenge, and change any debilitating assumptions you may not have even known you had until now. Our dream for your generation would be to see the public square filled with the next generation of influential Christians. Hopefully you will be able to count yourself in that group.

Knowing the goals of college freshmen helps make clear why the humanities have fallen on hard times. And this information helps explain why debates of our culture wars are so shallow, since the humanities are what train people to think carefully about important topics.

But why would Christians, with confidence in God's plan and provision, follow the secular culture in choosing a college major? In the past, a Christian went to college to discover his vocation—the area of service to which God has called him—and develop the skills necessary to occupy his place in the cultural and intellectual domain in a manner worthy of the kingdom of God. A believer would also go to college to gain general information and the habits of thought necessary for becoming a well-informed, good citizen of both earthly and heavenly kingdoms. Our public square may be devoid of influential Christians because they have abandoned the humanities, due to our culture's lack of appreciation for extrabiblical knowledge.

So, why do Christians continue to separate themselves from the intellectual world and ignore the value of the life of the mind?

WHY DO WE RESIST THE INTELLECTUAL LIFE?

Despite the evidence we've looked at from Scripture emphasizing the importance of the mind, some passages of the Bible are misunderstood and applied to actually support anti-intellectualism. Let's clear up these misconceptions in case you ever face any of them.

WE DISTORT 1 CORINTHIANS 1–2

In 1 Corinthians 1–2, the apostle Paul argues against the wisdom of the world and reminds his readers that he did not visit them with wise and persuasive words. Some have wrongly concluded that his contention means that reason and argument are pointless, particularly in regard to evangelism. Let's just say for a moment that this is what Paul meant—that argument and reason were futile when sharing the Christian faith. If so, then Paul's meaning would contradict his own practices in Acts as well as his stated desire (in the very same epistle) for believers to argue the evidence for the Resurrection (see 1 Corinthians 15).

This passage is more likely condemning a false and prideful use of reason, not reason itself. It is *hubris* (pride) that is the problem, not the *nous* (mind). God chose foolish *(moria)* things that were offensive to human pride to save mankind, but this does not mean God is opposed to reason properly used. For example, it is an offense to the prideful intellect to think that the greatest should be the servant of others, that strength comes through weakness, that giving your life away is the way to find it. The idea of God being crucified was so offensive that the Greeks would have judged it to be morally disgusting. Yet all these things are truly how God set up the world.

The passage may also be a condemnation of Greek rhetoric. Greek orators prided themselves on possessing persuasive words of wisdom. For the right price, they would persuade a crowd toward any side of an issue. They persuaded based on honed speaking abilities and not on the substance or merits of the arguments. (We would call this "spin" today.) If Paul is speaking to these folks, then he is also arguing against evangelists who focus on their speaking technique over the substance of their message.

WE DISTORT COLOSSIANS 2:8

In Colossians 2:8, Paul said, "See to it that no one takes you captive through hollow and deceptive philosophy, which depends on human tradition and the basic principles of this world rather than on Christ." Some people take this passage as a command to avoid studying secular subject matter (especially philosophy) or at least to downplay its importance to Christians. But when we look closer, we see that philosophy is not the enemy but a certain kind of philosophy— hollow and deceptive philosophy. If anything, this Scripture is a call to use our minds more boldly— to avoid heresy by having knowledge and thinking correctly.

Paul knew philosophy. Acts and Colossians reveal an apostle familiar enough with the current philosophy to refute it and use it to benefit his argument. We need to be like Paul. We must learn philosophy in order to discern faulty thinking and deceptive beliefs, using Scripture and right reason as a guide.

WE DISTORT ISAIAH 55:9 AND 1 CORINTHIANS 8:1

Some have argued that Isaiah 55:9 — "As the heavens are higher than the earth, so are my ways higher than your ways and my thoughts than your thoughts" — means it is futile to use reason. But whoever thought they could understand all of God's motives, purposes, and guidance anyway? To admit that we won't ever know what God knows says absolutely nothing about whether or not we should try to love and serve Him better with our minds. God is speaking about our arrogance as humans in believing that we could comprehend Him, so to use this passage as an excuse for ignorance or laziness wrongly twists the meaning of the verse.

First Corinthians 8:1 says, "Knowledge puffs up." This does not mean knowledge is bad and causes arrogance. Rather, our attitude toward knowledge is what Paul warned against. In humility, we must seek to learn and apply all of what God has revealed to us.

WE DISTORT FAITH TO BE A MATTER OF THE HEAD (AND NOT THE HEAD)

Recently, we met a believer who said, "I believe most people will miss heaven by eighteen inches." The remark was puzzling, so he elaborated: "Eighteen inches is roughly the distance from the head to the heart." We realized he meant that the heart (emotions) was superior to the head (reason). He cited as his support Jesus' teaching about the importance of being like little children in order to enter the kingdom of God (see Matthew 18:1-4).

Unfortunately, this opinion does not capture the substance of the teaching. In context, this teaching had nothing to do with the intellect. It was directed against being self-sufficient and arrogant. To be a child then is to be humble and willing to trust in or rely on others, especially God. The opposite is a proud, stiff-necked person, not an intelligent, reasonable one.

Further, the distinction between the head and the heart is misleading. In Scripture, the term *heart* has several meanings. Most of the time it refers to the total self, including intellect, emotion, and will. Sometimes it simply refers to the emotions or affections (see Romans 1:24; Philippians 1:8). And often it actually refers to the mind itself (see Romans 1:21; 2 Corinthians 4:6; 9:7; Ephesians 1:18). Therefore, it is safe to say that when the term *heart* is used in a verse, it most likely refers to our mind unless the context clearly shows otherwise.

And last, in Scripture, faith is relying on what you have reason to believe is true and trustworthy; that is, faith involves the readiness to act as if something were so. This brings to mind my (Mark's) rooftop "leap of faith." I did say I was ready to act, knowing (hoping!) God would make me fly. But here's where we find a distortion in my understanding of faith.

BACK TO THE ROOF

What was wrong with my faith? Was my heart not truly devoted to the belief that God was real and that my faith was sufficient to fly? No, my heart was quite devoted to the idea. I wanted to fly. Emotionally, I was ready to go — after all, I had made it to the roof of my house. But my heart-faith alone wasn't enough. What was missing was my mind-faith. Here's what I mean:

Throughout church history, theologians have expressed three different aspects of biblical faith: *notitia* (knowledge), *assensus* (assent), and *fiducia* (trust). *Notitia* refers to the data and doctrine of the Christian faith (see Jude 3). *Assensus* signifies agreement of the intellect with the truth of Christian teaching. These two aspects of faith require a careful exercise of reason, in both understanding what the teachings of Christianity are and judging their truthfulness. Reason is also required for the third aspect of faith — *fiducia* — which represents the personal application or trust involved (using the will, affections, *and* intellect).[7]

On the roof of my house, I had some *notitia:* First, faith as small as a mustard seed could move a mountain (see Matthew 17:20); therefore, the faith needed for me to fly would be less than a mustard seed. Second, if I remained in Christ, I could ask anything of Him and He would give it to me (see John 15:7); therefore, because I was walking with the Lord, surely He would grant my request.

But when it came to *assensus* — the agreement that God would allow this and that I was applying Scripture correctly — my faith broke down. I had some other knowledge: that God doesn't always give us what we want, even when we are walking closely with Him. I also knew that God wasn't into doing magic tricks and making a spectacle of His power. Jesus refused to perform a sign just for show when King Herod asked for one (see Luke 23:8-9)! My lack of *assensus* led to a lack of *fiducia.* I had very little trust that God would in fact honor my request.

Hebrews 11:1 says, "Now faith is being sure of what we hope for and certain of what we do not see." When it comes to my salvation, I have that confidence; jumping off of the roof, not so much. I am aware of the physical laws that govern my life, and I am aware that God can interrupt those physical laws if He so chooses. But God revealed to me that I can't defy those natural laws just because I believe He is real.

SMART THINKING

First, name the historical setting, main theme, and basic structure of at least one book of the Bible. If you can't do it, pick one that interests you now, make notes, and commit the information to memory. Learning this material will be easier if you tell someone what you learn. Practice on that person until you have it down.

Second, read *Sophie's World*,[8] a primer on philosophy, or another book on philosophy recommended by someone you respect for his knowledge. Be sure you don't just breeze through it. Challenge yourself so that after you are finished you can easily describe the core premise of several of the major philosophies.

CHAPTER THREE

WHAT DO WE KNOW?

MINDING OUR SOURCE FOR TRANSFORMATION

False ideas are the greatest obstacles to the reception of the gospel. We may preach with all the fervour of a reformer and yet succeed only in winning a straggler here and there, if we permit the whole collective thought of the nation or of the world to be controlled by ideas which, by the resistless force of logic, prevent Christianity from being regarded as anything more than a harmless delusion.

J. GRESHAM MACHEN

I (Mark) don't know about you, but as I worked with J. P. and learned about the significance of the intellect and our spiritual growth, I realized how underdeveloped my Christian mind is. Recognizing my intellectual shortcomings made me uncomfortable, to say the least. I wanted to change the situation right away. But being instantly transformed is not possible (as nice as that would be!). The development of our minds is a journey, and as long as we are continuing down the right path, we are moving in the right direction.

The information in chapters 1 and 2 is necessary to our journey, but now we need to know what to do with that information. We learned that there are problems in culture and the church due to anti-intellectualism, and we learned that the Bible includes solid arguments for developing our intellectual lives. Now we will examine what exactly the mind is and how it figures into our spiritual growth.

BE TRANSFORMED BY THE RENEWING OF OUR MINDS

To begin, let's take another look at Romans 12:1-2:

> I urge you, brethren, by the mercies of God, to present your bodies a living and holy sacrifice, acceptable to God, which is your spiritual service of worship. And do not be conformed to this world, but be transformed by the renewing of your mind, that you may prove what the will of God is, that which is good and acceptable and perfect. (Romans 12:1-2, NASB)

When Paul wrote these words, he zeroed in on how we grow to become like Jesus. This is arguably the most important text ever written about spiritual transformation. As we progress through this chapter, we will see how the term *renewing* (or *anakainosis* in the Greek, which means "making something new") describes what happens to our *mind* (or *nous* in the Greek, which means "intellect, reason, or faculty of understanding") when we incorporate new thoughts and beliefs.

In some ways, we are so familiar with verse 2 that we don't see how strange it is. For example, what about all the things Paul could have said but didn't: "Be transformed by developing close feelings toward God . . . by exercising your will in obeying biblical commands . . . by fellowship and worship," and so on. All of those are important parts of our Christian life, yet Paul chose none of them for his core guidance. So what is it about the mind that justifies the level of importance Paul gave it?

In verse 1, Paul reminds us that we should offer our bodies to God because this is the most reasonable way to express service to Him in light of His mercy toward us. Paul mentions the body for two reasons. First, it is our bodies we use to interact with the world. It is not enough to think about going for a bike ride; we must move our bodies to get the bike and take it for a spin. Second, our habits dwell in our bodies. We can get so into a routine that we do things without even thinking about them (like arriving home, throwing ourselves on the couch, and channel surfing). To change our habits and interact differently with the world, we must retrain our bodies to form new habits to replace the old.

But how do we gain the motivation? All of us have tried, with differing levels of success, to get rid of bad habits and create good habits. We know that we don't become transformed just by hoping the old will go away or the new will come easily. Even with strong willpower, we fail. And, unfortunately, this is what the church often tells us: what we should be doing but not how to do it.

According to Paul, the key to change is obtaining a new perspective—that is, fresh insight about our lives and the world as well as the knowledge and skill required to know what to do and how to do it. Paul's teaching was not new. The Old Testament is filled with the same idea about the role of wisdom in life. It asks us to think carefully because God has put reason all around us:

"Do you know the ordinances of the heavens, . . .

Who has put wisdom in the innermost being,

Or has given understanding to the mind?" (Job 38:33,36, NASB)

We can find knowledge and wisdom (see Psalm 119) in the natural world and its operations (see Isaiah 28:23-29) and in the insight embedded in the art, literature, and science of different cultures (see Isaiah 19:11-13; Jeremiah 49:7; Daniel 2:12-13; 5:7). But the Old Testament also warns us that knowledge and wisdom come to only those who are diligent in their pursuit of it:

Make your ear attentive to wisdom,

Incline your heart to understanding. (Proverbs 2:2, NASB)

Seek [wisdom] as silver

And search for her as for hidden treasures. (Proverbs 2:4, NASB)

These verses tell us we have to work hard at using our minds to seek truth, with a life of wisdom and virtue as our goal. And in order to leverage the truth we find for transformation, we need to understand the inner workings of our minds.

BODY AND SOUL

When my (J. P.'s) daughter Allison was in the sixth grade, she came to me complaining that if she could only see God (say, sitting in a chair), then prayer would be much easier. I pointed out that not only had she never seen God but she had never seen me either. She gave me a look.

I told her she could see my body, but she could not see my "I," my self, my ego, nor could she see my thoughts, feelings, and so on. Yet those things are who I truly am. People, I told her, are invisible objects, and because God is too big to have a body, He cannot be seen in the same way as a chair or a person's body.[9] This is the Christian understanding of human beings. In history and the Bible, Christianity includes a *dualistic* interpretation of a human being; each of us is made up of the union of two distinct realities: body and soul.[10]

You see, you *are* your soul and you *have* a body. In *substance dualism* theology, the soul is not immortal by nature but is capable of entering a disembodied state upon death where it waits to eventually be reunited with a resurrected body.

DEFINING THE SOUL

The soul (that is, the self, or the "I") is that immaterial and invisible thing that makes me a conscious, living human being. When I am aware of what is going on inside me, I go where the soul resides. If God took my soul and put it into your body and placed your soul into my body, we would have different bodies. Many movies have toyed with this idea of having two people switch bodies.

Okay, you might be thinking, *but what about all those words in Scripture—like soul, spirit, heart, and mind—that seem to have similar meanings?* Well, in Scripture,

- *Soul* can refer to the total person, including the body (see Genesis 2:7, KJV; Psalm 63:1), or it can refer to the total immaterial self, or "I," which can survive the destruction of the body (see Matthew 10:28; John 12:25). It contains desires (see 2 Samuel 3:21) and emotions (see Psalm 119:28) and is what knows (see Psalm 139:14) and exercises the will to do something (see Psalm 130:6; 119:129).
- Sometimes *spirit* is used as a synonym for *soul*. But *spirit* also refers to the aspect of human beings that relates to God (see Psalm 51:10; Romans 8:16; Ephesians 4:23).
- *Heart* refers to the center of human personality (see Proverbs 4:32), in which case it is equivalent to the *soul*. At other times, *heart* signifies the basis of our will and desire (see Exodus 35:5; Deuteronomy 8:2; Romans 2:5),

of feelings (see Proverbs 14:30; 23:17), and of thought
and reason (see Deuteronomy 29:4; Psalm 90:12; Isaiah
65:17).

- *Mind* is that which reasons and thinks (see Romans 14:5;
  Philippians 4:8; Colossians 3:2).

With these definitions in mind, we can develop a map of the soul.
Knowing what our soul is and how it works will help us understand
how to grow in different aspects of our faith. Just as God is present
everywhere, our soul is fully present within the entirety of our bodies.
The soul and the body relate to one another in a seamless and intimate cause-and-effect way. For example, if I worry in my soul, my
brain chemistry will change. If I exercise my will to raise my arm, my
hand also goes up. If my hand is placed on a hot object, my soul will
be more conscious to avoid the same pain in the future.

SOUL "STATES" AND "FACULTIES"

The soul contains various "states," such as sensations, thoughts, beliefs,
desires, and acts of the will. There are more states of the soul, but these
five are primary. As an example, think for a moment of states of the
soul as H_2O. The molecular structure of H_2O is two parts hydrogen
and one part oxygen, yet it is sometimes in a state of liquid (water),
solid (ice), or gas (steam). Likewise, the soul can be in a sensing,
thinking, or believing state but still be the same entity.

The soul also includes "faculties," which are much more numerous
than the states. A soul's faculty is a grouping of various potentialities
or capacities within the soul that are not being utilized or realized
at any given moment. When I (Mark) was a little kid, I had a frog
hatchery kit that allowed me to observe the life cycle of a frog. Once
I had the kit set up, I sent away for a free set of frog eggs. The eggs
arrived in a little container, and I waited with great anticipation for

them to hatch. It was magic for me to believe that a frog could come from this little translucent egg.

Anyway, the egg had multiple capacities, foremost of which was to become a frog. But before the egg could become a frog, it had several stages to go through. I found that out the hard way. When the eggs hatched, I was disappointed. This thing wasn't a frog! It was a tadpole—just a head and tail.

The tadpole, too, had various capacities, one of which was to live both in the water and on the land—but not yet. The tadpole had no legs. The frog's ultimate capacity could be achieved only after certain levels of development occurred—not to mention in the right order and in the right manner. Waiting for that frog was one of my early lessons in patience.

The adult human soul has thousands of capacities—many more than a frog—that make up our faculties. Here are some faculties: ability to see red, ability to talk to God, ability to see shapes, ability to will your hand to lift, ability to think about math, desire to eat lunch, and desire to fall in love. Now, it should be obvious that the ability to see red is more closely related to the ability to see shapes than it is to think about math. This is because these are related to the same faculty of sight. Thinking about math would fall into the faculty of thought.

All of a soul's capacities to see are part of the faculty of sight. This is important because if your eyeballs are defective to the point of blindness, then your soul's faculty of sight will be inoperative, just as a car won't start if the spark plugs are not in working order. Likewise, if your eyes are working (reading a book) but your soul is not in a thinking state (daydreaming), then you also won't see what is before you. So as your conscious inner life changes from one moment to the next, the different faculties of the soul go from one state to another. The mind may change from the state of thinking about lunch to thinking about the weekend. The faculty of emotion may change from a state of anxiety to one of anger. And so on.

I (Mark) had a friend who attended the same school and had the same teachers his older siblings did. But his grades did not reflect the same level of achievement. Was he just not as smart as the others? He wasn't lazy, and he had a lot of talent, yet he struggled in school. Incentives and punishment seemed to have little effect. Once he reached high school, a wise teacher noticed he was not living up to his capacities. She took a different approach. After having him take various tests, she realized he was missing some basic language skills. She put him through remedial reading and writing exercises, and within a year his performance in school had remarkably improved. You see, before he could experience growth on a higher order, he had to have some lower-order capacities in place.

The same is true of our spiritual transformation. Until certain faculties of the soul are developed, we cannot reach new levels or ultimately our full potential in the Christian life. And when one faculty of the soul is stunted, it can have a negative effect on other faculties. But rather than see this fact as discouraging, we should view it as empowering; that is, when God shows us a troubled faculty of our soul (such as low self-esteem), we can then do what's necessary (such as seeking counsel) so that a handicapped spiritual faculty (the inability to approach God without shame) is free to develop in a positive direction.

The influence goes both ways. This means that as our spirit matures, it can exert a great positive influence on other faculties of the soul. The focus of this book is to liberate the faculty of our minds so that it will stop hindering and instead fire up our spiritual growth.

POWER HIDDEN IN OUR MINDS

One of the most obvious transitions we experience in life is from a child to an adult. Bridging those stages is the one we know as *adolescence*, similar to the maturity of our faith from spiritual infancy to a complete maturity (see Hebrews 5:11-14; Ephesians 4:13; James 1:4). Most of us had no problem putting away the flannel-graph Bible stories and the VeggieTales to step deeper into our understanding of Christ. And most of us definitely reached spiritual adolescence. But is it possible that since then our level of maturity hasn't increased very much? Times when we have a feeling that there's not much further to go in our spiritual walk or that we need to go further but don't know how are signals that we're stuck and need to do some digging into the faculty of our minds. The writer of Hebrews admonishes us,

> Solid food is for the mature, who by constant use have trained themselves to distinguish good from evil. Therefore let us leave the elementary teachings about Christ and go on to maturity. (5:14–6:1)

We're familiar with this admonition, but what is "solid food," and how do we "go on to maturity"? Well, the mind is the part of the soul with thoughts and beliefs, and the spirit is that part of the soul through which we relate to God. He puts capacities in us at our new birth to change our souls. We must nourish these numerous untapped capacities of the mind—that is, "eat" the "solid food." This use of our minds combined with Christ's work in us will help us "go on to maturity."

One of those capacities of the mind that strongly influence us is our beliefs. *Beliefs* are the rails upon which our lives run. We almost always act according to what we really believe. That is why behavior is a good indicator of what a person believes. In the same way that a physically damaged brain can limit the soul's ability to think and hold beliefs, an inattentive or underused mind will limit our ability to think deeply or hold well-defended beliefs. This lack can make Christians and Christianity appear very weak. So let's explore what a belief is made of.

I (Mark) have been doing research for several years now. Most of this research has involved polling students about their beliefs. During the survey many students would tell the surveyor they believe something, but once we ask them how strongly they believed it, we found that the belief lacked any strength. For instance, when we asked students if they believed there was a spiritual dimension beyond what our five senses could detect, 73 percent said they believed such a dimension existed. Yet when we asked them how strongly they believed this, only 41 percent were confident in their belief. Of the 22 percent who said there was no spiritual dimension, only 8 percent were confident of their belief.[11] So can a statement about something truly be considered a belief when there is no strength of conviction? If we dissect a belief in the way we dissect frogs in biology class, we would find four parts. The anatomy of a belief is content, strength, centrality, and plausibility.

CONTENT OF A BELIEF

The *content of a belief* determines what we believe. The content may include what we believe about God, morality, politics, life after death, and so on. The content shapes our lives and our actions. A person's beliefs are so important that, according to Scripture, our eternal destiny is determined by what we believe about Jesus Christ.

By the way people behave today, it would seem that the sincerity or fervency of their beliefs is more important than the content. If we believe that grape jelly will fuel our cars better than gasoline, we can believe that as strongly as we want, but the car isn't going anywhere. Reality doesn't care how fervently we believe something. What matters is not whether we strongly believe but whether what we believe is true or not. Just as electricity was real but its power unavailable to us until Ben Franklin's discovery opened our minds to grasp the true nature of electricity, so the power of the spiritual life is real but unavailable to us if we don't understand the true nature of prayer, fasting, or any other spiritual discipline. This is why truth is so powerful. It allows us to cooperate with reality, whether spiritual or physical, and tap into its power.

We've all heard people say they live basically good lives and that they don't believe God will really allow anyone to go to hell. They can believe this all they want to, but the Bible and the natural world point toward the reality of punishment for wrongdoing as well as the reality that Christ is the only way to escape that punishment and find life. There is more reasonable evidence to support punishment than no punishment. So, no matter how much people believe being good is a measure for eternal life, if this content is not true, it isn't worth believing. The content of a belief will shape your life whether the content is true or not.

STRENGTH OF A BELIEF

There is more to a belief than its content, however. Even if a polled student chose a true answer, if she doesn't have conviction about the answer, then it won't likely make an impact on her life. To have *strength of conviction*, we must be more than 50 percent convinced it is true. If we are fifty-fifty even, we wouldn't yet strongly hold the belief. Instead, we would be thinking the belief is probably true but still deciding. As we gain evidence and support for a belief, its strength will grow. The belief may start off as plausible and then become fairly likely, quite likely, beyond reasonable doubt, until finally, completely certain.

For most of my life, I (Mark) had no problem believing that Jesus rose from the dead. I never questioned this important aspect of my faith. Incredibly, I got as far as graduating from college without anyone challenging my belief. Well, at that point, I was preparing a message on the resurrection of Christ and began to read books by people who had examined this subject in depth. The reasonable and rational evidence for the Resurrection amazed me! My soul shifted with transformation: Based on the evidence I had researched, the strength of my belief increased. Interestingly, I never would have characterized my belief as weak (sometimes we don't know we're missing something), but by stimulating my mind, confidence and boldness resulted—in my faith, my life, and my ministry. The more we are certain of a belief, the more the belief becomes a part of our very soul, and the more we rely on the belief as a basis for action.

CENTRALITY OF A BELIEF

Content of a belief and strength of a belief may seem pretty obvious, but the *centrality of a belief* is more subtle. The centrality of a belief is the degree of importance the belief plays in our entire set of beliefs—that is, in our worldview. The more central a belief is, the greater the impact it will make in our daily life.

For example, most people would agree based on substantial evidence that exercise is good for us. And many people personally believe exercise is good for them. So one would expect to find more people at the gym and fewer obese people, yet we don't. In fact, obesity is a growing problem in our nation. Even when people hold true content (exercise is good for them) and strength to the belief (little question that it is true), if the belief is not a central belief in their lives, then they won't be rushing to go work out. Now, a person may become ill or have a situation arise that moves exercise to the center of his life, but for now, if the belief isn't central, then the person won't act on it.

Many Christians hold true beliefs about God, feel more than 50 percent strong in their conviction, but their beliefs are not central to their lives. This means their beliefs about God have little impact on how they live each day.

PLAUSIBILITY OF A BELIEF

Along with beliefs, our minds measure the world through *plausibility*. Many great movies are based on convincing the viewer of the plausibility of the central concept for the story. *Jurassic Park,* for instance, would have failed (even with the impressive special effects) if the viewer was not convinced that dinosaurs could be genetically engineered. Seeing is not believing; the storyteller had to create a world in which we could believe this far-fetched idea. Some are more easily convinced than others. We've all known "fantasy killers," the people who refuse to buy into the world presented in the story. These people continually point out plot and credibility gaps. To be believable, an idea must be plausible. For instance, if a friend approached you with the idea that the earth is flat, you wouldn't even entertain such a notion. Our culture and society has so deeply accepted the concept that earth is round that any argument supporting a flat earth is viewed as too ridiculous to even consider.

Slavery of African-Americans provides a more serious example. An honest examination of the practice finds it wrong on all counts. Slavery blatantly contradicted the values of our nation: equality, life, liberty, and the pursuit of happiness. How could the hypocrisy survive? The plausibility structure of our nation during that era offers one answer: At that time, many people did not consider slaves human beings, so the plausibility of slaves possessing rights on par with nonslaves was incomprehensible. The truth that slaves *were* human beings was not part of their plausibility structure until many thinking people began to realize the incongruities.

This issue still survives today, albeit with a different name. *Racism* is just one social injustice that dramatically shows how entrenched plausibility structures can become not only in one individual but throughout an entire nation. Plausibility structures in society may require generations to change, but you are one individual, and your plausibility structures can change in your lifetime—depending on whether you stop to examine them.

Unfortunately, the plausibility structure surrounding Christianity has changed to its detriment. At one time in America, belief in God and the authority of Scripture was considered plausible. That is not so today. Many factors have changed our plausibility structure, but one event marked a turning point. In the 1925 Scopes Monkey Trial, creation and evolution theories were put on trial. Because the Christian mind had already been weakened and because Christians thus offered few reasonable arguments to support creationism, the faith was made a mockery.

If a culture reaches a point where the beliefs of Christianity are no longer part of its plausibility structure, fewer and fewer people will be able to even entertain the idea that the beliefs are true.

THE PATH OF TRANSFORMATION

So the transformation of the mind requires more than merely the discovery of a truth. That truth must be plausible, we must believe it to be true, and we must be able to support that truth with conviction. Finally, we must make the truth central where it can make an impact on our daily lives.

Did you ever think that changing your beliefs would be so difficult? We can't just change our mind about something. Yet Scripture holds us accountable for what we believe and also warns us about ideas we should not believe.

When I (Mark) was in high school, I was arrogant when it came to issues about God. I knew many unbelievers, and I made sure to inform them that if they didn't see things my way, well, they were ignorant pagans doomed to hellfire. Even though I had gone to church for most of my life, I never really examined Jesus until my senior year. As

I evaluated His interactions with others, it became glaringly clear that He treated everyone quite differently than I did. For the first time, I understood sin and how Jesus had saved me from it. I also realized God's grace, even though I had already received it. This awakening of my mind stopped me in my tracks. I did a one-eighty in the way I interacted with people. I learned to reach out in a loving and gracious way to others while still proclaiming the truth.

So, if we want to change our beliefs about a subject, we can begin a course of study in which we (1) choose to think regularly about the subject, (2) consider certain pieces of evidence and arguments in support of it, (3) consider certain pieces of evidence and arguments against it, and (4) analyze the strengths and weaknesses of the arguments both for and against.

THE MIND AND SEEING

Have you ever taken a moment to consider what it means to see? It's easy to take sight for granted. We walk through life seeing many things, but sometimes we lack real "sight." For instance, we may see a couple hugging at the airport and assume they are romantically connected when in actuality they are brother and sister. The physical reality of sight isn't all there is to seeing. The mind plays an important role in determining what a person is able to see, and how we see is significant to our reasoning abilities.

Philosophers distinguish between three kinds of seeing. First we have *simple seeing:* for example, having a dog directly in our visual field and noticing it. We don't need to have a concept of what a dog is to see one. We also don't need to be thinking about a dog to see it. And we can later recall details about a dog we've seen, such as its color.

Second we have *seeing as.* In this case, we see an object as being something or other. We can see a dog as a dog or as my neighbor's favorite pet. *Seeing as* involves classifying the object of sight as a mental concept. Mental concepts are located in the mind, which means that *seeing as* needs our eyes and minds working together. When we see a dog as a dog, we must have some concept of what a dog is and apply this to the object we are seeing. Once when my (Mark's) son was visiting my workplace, he became fascinated with the paper shredder. I gave him some paper to shred, but later I came out of my office and panicked because he was shredding twenty-dollar bills! He merely saw paper as paper. The concept of money was not yet developed in his mind. And I saw the paper as a twenty-dollar bill!

Third, there is *seeing that.* With this type of seeing, a person judges with his mind that some perceptual belief is true. I saw that the paper had value, so I grabbed the remaining bills out of my son's hand. But once I saw the bills close up, I realized they were play money and that they had no value after all.

Simple seeing involves only the faculty of vision. With simple seeing, there is no interpretation of what you see; there is only the direct awareness of the object. For example, a child may simply be aware of an apple without having any concept of what an apple is. But *seeing as* and *seeing that* involve the mind. This is why the more one knows, the more one can see. If we have two people grocery shopping—one who has been to culinary school and one who has not—the one who has more culinary knowledge will be able to "see" much more in the available products. The one who knows more will see ten varieties of greens (and be able to name them and use them in different dishes), while the other person will overlook the differences and see only greens.

Let's take this a step further. We often read the Bible, hear the news, listen to a sermon, or talk to friends, yet we don't get much out of it. One central reason for this may be our lack of knowledge. The more we know, the more we see and hear because our minds bring more to the task of *seeing as* or *seeing that.* In fact, the more we know about the Bible and extrabiblical matters, the more we will see in the Bible. That's because revelation in the Bible that was previously invisible to us will become visible as we add new concepts to our minds.

But it's easy to fall into unproductive habits, which means renewing our minds is critical to our spiritual growth. During a chapel program I attended at Biola University, a professor from the intercultural studies program showed us photographs from the Filipino culture. He asked us to make some observations about what we had seen. After some had shared their observations, the professor then gave us some information about the Filipino people regarding how they lived and how they thought. He went through each photo and explained how our observations had been wrong because we were viewing them from an American perspective and not as Filipinos! This was a great illustration of how our minds get into ruts and cannot get out without the introduction of fresh perspectives and ideas. A life devoted to study and learning keeps our minds fresh and alert to seeing new insights.

SMART THINKING

> What do you believe? Here is a short list of common beliefs (we've supplied the content). Write *1, 2, 3, 4,* or *5* (*1* being weakest, *5* being strongest) next to each belief to indicate how strongly you hold the belief. Next write how central this belief is to your life, using *core* for "major impact," *middle* for "some impact," and *outer* for "little impact." The first one is an example.
>
> <u>5, outer</u> Exercise is good for me.
>
> _____ Using tobacco is not healthy.

_____ Jesus never sinned while He was on earth.

_____ Sex is for marriage only.

_____ All people are good.

_____ Watching too much television is bad for me.

_____ Abortion is murder.

_____ God is always good.

_____ Mary was a virgin when she became pregnant with Jesus.

_____ Satan is a real, living spiritual being.

_____ Jesus rose from the dead.

_____ God created the earth and all of earth's creatures.

_____ I have a responsibility to tell others about Jesus.

Now review your responses. Are there some beliefs you feel should be stronger? Can you defend why you believe strongly those you marked with a 4 or 5? Should any beliefs you marked as middle or outer be core? Focus on two or three beliefs you want to change in some way and then begin an investigation by asking God to work in you as you collect knowledge, study your Bible, and seek wise counsel.

CHAPTER FOUR

BRAIN FREEZE

MELTING OUR MENTAL ICEBERGS

Christians must avoid the intellectual flabbiness of the larger society. They must rally against the prevailing distrust of reason and the exaltation of the irrational. Emotional self-indulgence and irrationalities have always been the enemies of the gospel, and the apostles warned their followers against them.

HERBERT SCHLOSSBERG

No doubt you have experienced brain freeze, the unpleasant sensation of eating ice cream too fast and the cold causing an intense pain in your head. Acting natural is difficult when this occurs. Typically you make an unintelligible sound, tighten your face into an awful contortion, and definitely stop eating the ice cream until the agony passes. During the prolonged burst, you are unable to focus on anything but the pain.

Imagine living most of your life with your mind numbed by brain freeze. While we may not experience the physical pain, our culture experiences brain freeze as a continual suspension of deeper thinking. Brain freeze causes us to think of nothing but ourselves.

However, to be a part of spiritual power and productivity for the

kingdom of God, our intellectual life requires self-denial and dedication. Jesus taught that spending all of our time looking at ourselves
makes it impossible to focus on what life is really about. But if we
deny ourselves daily for Christ's sake—that is, if we stop focusing
on ourselves and stare at Him with dedication and affection—we
are able to see our own lives more clearly and in the right context
(see Matthew 16:24-27). The purpose of our lives is to bring honor
to God—to know Him, love Him, obey Him, become like Him, and
live for His purposes in this world as we prepare to live in the next
one. If we are to live for this purpose, we must regularly die to focusing on ourselves for the good of ourselves and the body of Christ. We
must live for the kingdom of God and be involved aggressively in the
war between that kingdom and the kingdom of darkness.

While self-interest and personal joy are important aspects of our
faith, alone they are not adequate to make a skillful Christian life. We
must also seek to live for others. This is the true good life. Our culture
communicates an entirely different good life, one we're sure you can
describe. But the true good life is not easy. It requires discipline, hard
work, suffering, patience, and endurance in forming habits and virtues
characteristic of Christ. Just like all challenges that end in reward, a
better understanding of and closer relationship with God will be well
worth your effort.

Learning to melt brain freeze before it takes over our lives is the
goal of this chapter. But the Devil loves to use things in our culture
that make us feel good to coax us into a state of brain freeze. In
the following section, we've presented the primary lures in life that
produce brain freeze as well as several strategies to keep our minds
warm and functioning at an optimum level.

First we'll look at three enemies to the Christian mind that wield a
broad power if Christians let them. We want you to keep these in mind
at all times, knowing they are working against your commitment to

follow Christ. Second, we'll look at a mind-set called "the empty self," learn how it negatively shapes our intellectual habits, and then learn how to develop healthy habits instead. These healthy habits will prevent your mind from becoming a frozen wasteland and help lead you to greater fulfillment in your Christian walk.

THIEVES OF OUR CHRISTIAN MINDS

Be vigilant as you watch for these thieves that will often attempt to steal your growth and joy. Look to Christ for help to capture and subdue these bad guys.

INSECURITY

If we feel our mental capabilities are lacking, it's difficult to have confidence in them. The possibility of being embarrassed or looking stupid in front of others can often keep us from pursuing intellectual goals and interactions. The fear of ridicule is a real one.

One young woman we know mentioned in a group that the sun orbited the earth. (The truth is, of course, that the earth orbits the sun.) No one corrected her, which on the one hand saved her some embarrassment but on the other hand made her feel she had said something true. Embarrassing someone or reinforcing an incorrect belief is not loving, but offering someone the truth in love is the way to go. We later gently corrected her in such a way as to avoid embarrassment and help her grow in understanding.

This simple illustration shows how difficult it might be for someone to grow in his knowledge and understanding of God without taking some risks and interacting with others on subjects of faith. Maybe you have been embarrassed in class or another person has made you feel stupid. If you allow yourself to draw inward and avoid interaction, know that you're adopting a life that doesn't pursue intellectual development. You are missing out!

In our quest for intellectual and spiritual growth, we must treat our brothers and sisters in Christ (and all people) with respect. Doing so will minimize the fear we all have when sharing with one another.

We can't gain confidence without putting ourselves out there. I (Mark) wouldn't know half of what I do if I didn't offer up my ideas and filter through the reactions. That is how we grow. (And by the way, though hashing over various ideas with a group of friends might appear intimidating right now, give it a try. When we stop worrying about feeling stupid, we find out that the process can be fun.)

PRIDE

When we do feel insecure, a common defense mechanism is to become "puffed up" so as to appear supremely knowledgeable to others. Possessing this pride damages our relationship with God, blocks our learning, and causes us to be unkind to others. If right now you seem to know more than others around you, praise God! Use that knowledge to help others grow. Ask yourself how you can serve them with what you know. But maybe you've also heard the saying, "The more you know, the more you realize you don't know." Seek humility. It is essential to the Christian life and to developing a healthy intellect.

CONTROL

I (J. P.) once told my daughters that if they ever got to the point where they thought it was unreasonable to believe that Christianity was true, then they should abandon the faith. Would your parents say the same thing? That's a huge risk, isn't it? It is, but the unspoken alternative is worse: "Believe what I do and accept Christianity without using your intelligence." That doesn't make sense! Yet many parents are communicating just that, even if they're not using those exact words.

With that pressure in mind, is rebellion among children from

Christian families any surprise? Many people who have grown up in a Christian home are discouraged from thinking because some of the authorities in their lives (parents, teachers, pastors) are afraid to lose control of the outcome. Ironically, control is usually lost anyway. But you don't have to rebel or walk away from your faith if you come from a control-oriented family or church. If we truly believe that God is rational and engages the mind, we should have nothing to fear from anyone's challenge or inquiry. A loved one's doubt may unnerve us, and we may not have the answer (yet) he or she is seeking, but God is certainly not worried. He stands unmoving behind His truth. So let go of how you expect someone to respond to you and your faith. Trust God to help you handle that person's response, your own feelings, and any actions you might take (such as research into the subject) because of the response. Doing so will be a weight off your shoulders.

FROZEN WASTELAND

What psychologists refer to as the empty self has frozen much of our postmodern culture. The empty self is made up of values, motives, and habits of thought, feeling, and behavior that twist and kill the life of the mind and make spiritual maturity difficult. Let's examine the primary traits of the empty self that undermine intellectual and spiritual growth.

If some of these seem extreme, just remember that at different times in life, we all exhibit attitudes of the empty self. You will see different aspects of yourself in the traits. Not to worry—you're normal. But after this, you will know some areas in which you can improve, inviting God to work His transformation in you.

THE EMPTY SELF LOOKS OUT FOR NUMBER ONE

Recently, the small group of teenagers that met in my (Mark's) house was asked to talk about why they would wait until they were married to have sex. We had just completed a biblical examination of purity and holiness, and I was curious to hear their responses. Before I heard their responses, I made a mental prediction based on what I know about self-interest—that all of the reasons would refer to the personal benefits of waiting until they were married to have sex.

Sure enough, students began sharing about the diseases they might get, how embarrassing it would be if they broke up with their sex partner and that person revealed private information, and the risk of pregnancy. Perhaps you would answer in the same way. It's not that those are bad reasons for waiting to have sex. They are good reasons, but there is something more. What was missing from their discussion was any sort of virtue or matter of duty to their future spouse! Nobody talked about premarital sex as being an experience that would bring shame to those involved, their families, and God. Nobody talked about waiting to experience sex within marriage because that is the right and virtuous and obedient thing to do. Individual and self-focused reasons were the only ones given.

Now, a healthy form of individualism is a good thing. We all know people without it—those who go along with the crowd and cannot think for themselves. They are easy to manipulate, and they are too dependent on what others think of them. The healthy individual, on the other hand, maintains his identity but also learns to mutually depend on other members of the body of Christ. This type of individualism produces strong persons who have the power to practice self-denial to enrich the broader group (such as family and church) of which they are a part.

Watch out for the empty self that defines its values, life goals, and morals as if it were in a bubble isolated from others without responsibility toward the community. Self-contained individuals do their own thing and seek to find meaning only by looking into their own selves. As psychologist Martin Seligman warns, "The self is a very poor site for finding meaning."[12]

THE EMPTY SELF IS CHILDISH

Do your parents ever try to act younger than they are? Do they try to use cool words, dress a certain way, or adopt a younger hairstyle (or hair color) but just can't seem to pull it off? There is a powerful pressure in today's society to stay younger longer. Nobody wants to grow old and go through the process of becoming wise and mature. After all, those people aren't having fun, and we'd rather have it all right now!

This is an example of how the childish empty self behaves. It seeks instant gratification, comfort, and soothing—just like a baby. Think about the pettiness that sometimes appears in people at Christmastime. For some reason when relatives gather, people become childish and self-centered. Feelings get hurt for the most bizarre reasons.

The childish person is controlled by infantile cravings and seeks fulfillment with food, entertainment, and consumer goods. Such a person is preoccupied with sex, physical appearance, and body image and tends to live by feelings and experiences. For the childish empty self, pain, hard work, and discipline are avoided at all costs. Immediate and easily accessible pleasure is all that matters. Boredom is the greatest evil, and amusement is the greatest good.

THE EMPTY SELF IS SELF-ABSORBED

Another word for self-absorption is narcissism. Narcissism is an overload of self-infatuation in which a person is preoccupied with self-interest and personal fulfillment.[13] Narcissists manipulate relationships with others, including God, to validate their own self-esteem. They cannot sustain deep attachments or make personal commitments to something larger than their own ego (a likely reason why so many Hollywood marriages don't last!).

The Christian narcissist brings a Copernican revolution to the Christian faith. Let us explain. The Copernican Revolution dethroned the earth from the center of the universe and put the sun in its place. Spiritually, the narcissist dethrones God and His purpose in history from the center of life and replaces Him with her own personal fulfillment. So, a narcissist chooses his church, books, entertainment, exercise program, friends, and so on depending on what he gets out of the experience rather than on how he can give of himself to a greater purpose, such as God's.

THE EMPTY SELF IS A COUCH POTATO

The couch potato is a role model for those who are passive in their approach to life. We often let other people do our living and our thinking for us. The pastor does our Bible study, the media does our political thinking, and our favorite sports teams do the exercise while we just paint our blubbery selves with their insignias.

Proverbs reminds us, "He who loves pleasure will become poor" (21:17). From watching television to listening to a sermon, the primary goal of the empty self is be entertained. Holidays used to be considered "holy days," a valuable change of pace in which play, fellowship, and recreation refreshed our souls. Now we have *vacation*, which is derived from the word *vacate*, and that is what the empty self does: vacates its normal life to be amused, often returning to normal life more exhausted than when it left.

Television, movies, and video games are major culprits in creating passivity in life. While we believe there is nothing inherently wrong with any of these media, the amount of time that is spent indulging in them is a problem. Studies indicate that the amount of television viewing in America leads to mental passivity, reduces motivation and the ability to stick with something, negatively affects reading skills (especially those needed for higher-level mental comprehension), weakens the ability to listen and stay focused, and encourages overall passive withdrawal from life.[14] As we become intertwined with celebrities and sports figures, we cease to have lives of our own and begin to live our lives through others.

THE EMPTY SELF IS SENSUAL

The sensual self is one who bases her decisions not on careful, abstract reasoning on pertinent issues but on sense images. For example, advertisements sell us items based on images, not on thoughtful content about the product. We often buy something because, well, the image of it seems good.

Our generation increasingly fits this description of the empty self. Previous generations were more able to reason carefully, in part, because their culture was based on writing and abstract ideas, not on images. In a book called *The Crisis of Our Age*, Harvard sociologist Pitirim A. Sorokin claimed that cultures come in two major types: sensate and ideational. The sensate culture believes the physical world that can be experienced with the five senses is pretty much all there is.[15] (Sounds like Hume and Kant, huh?) This type of a culture is intensely secular. The ideational culture believes there is much more to be experienced than just what can be experienced sensually—such as virtues, morals, and abstract items like numbers and propositions (statements of truth).

As we discussed in chapter 1, our society has become primarily sensate and secular. Sorokin believed that a sensate culture will eventually disintegrate because it lacks the intellectual resources necessary to sustain a public and private life conducive to corporate and individual human flourishing.[16] Christians can and should play a critical role in bringing back an ideational culture.

THE EMPTY SELF DOES NOT LOOK INWARD

There are two aspects of our lives: the exterior life we live outside the body, and the interior life that is personal and private. The interior life is the world of the soul and the mind. We often do many things to improve our existence in the world we live with others, but we rarely take time to develop and improve our interior life, where we reason, think, and make decisions about what we believe. Living for the senses makes the interior world seem mundane and unnecessary. Yet the development of the inner self is what brings great joy and peace to our lives.

At one time, the self was a description of one's character, beliefs, and thoughts. In the last several decades, the definition of self has shifted to what a person looks like: the clothes she wears, the location of her home, and what possessions she has. Presidents are selected more on their likeability than on the content of their ideas. And celebrities complain that nobody really knows who they are as people.

THE EMPTY SELF IS BUSY

Modern life is filled with activity, but little of this hectic life is essential for living. Even elementary school children are busy, rushing from school to gymnastics, music lessons, and church activities and then doing schoolwork. Kids don't free-form play anymore; they have "play dates."

Many of us have a lurking fear that if we don't fill our lives with activity, we won't progress far in life or, worse, we'll sit in a chair long enough to realize how empty our lives really are. This fear is a powerful tool of the Enemy and in opposition to the truth. Hurried activity and constant distraction block intellectual development, which requires time to be still and reflect. If we are to allow our minds to mature in our faith, we must slow down. This may seem impossible, even unrealistic, but we must take steps to make that happen, counting on God to help bring order and boundaries to our lives.

I (Mark) really appreciate my parents. They made my childhood and adolescence significant by keeping me from becoming too busy with activities, and they never required me to get a job when I was in high school (though I did have responsibilities at home). Of course, many students today work for the stuff they want that their parents can't afford. But we should ask ourselves, *Doesn't that put us on a constant treadmill of wanting material things we don't really need and that don't really help us mature—working hard to get them, finding them less than fulfilling, and then wanting something else and starting all over again?*

WHY EMPTY SELVES ARE DANGEROUS TO THE CHURCH

A society filled with empty selves will have a difficult time determining what is moral. The society will also be devoid of intellect and painfully shallow. An example of this is the approach to the abortion debate. Few regard this issue from a thoughtful analysis of relevant arguments. Instead, people focus on what abortion does or does not do for them. For example, single people may use sex to try to fill their empty selves. Then when a woman becomes pregnant, the couple may justify an abortion because it allows them to continue with their "right" to have sex without responsibility whenever and with whomever they please.

What may be worse is a church full of empty selves incapable of articulating abortion arguments without the use of Scripture. It is pretty obvious that it is wrong to intentionally kill innocent human beings. For example, it would be wrong to kill a three-month-old baby just because its parent didn't want it. Well, it's also obvious that the baby in the womb is an innocent human being. He or she isn't a goldfish! And the baby has done nothing wrong. The conclusion is obvious. The morality of abortion is virtually self-evident, yet Christians have turned abortion into a religious debate rather than one based solely on morality and ethics that appeal to those who choose not to believe in God.

THAWING OUR EMPTY SELVES

The sad reality is, many of us have ignorantly adopted a lifestyle of the empty self. Because people are part of this empty culture not just in church but in our neighborhoods and schools, the problem is a challenge to solve. We must live in our world but not be of it (John 17:15-18), and that is not easy to do. There are no easy or quick fixes. This circumstance means we need Christians (you!) with a far-reaching perspective to look to the future, move in the right direction, and start a shift. We believe the battle for the mind will be ultimately won or lost depending on how we change the habits of the empty self.

EVALUATE OURSELVES HONESTLY

If we cannot honestly examine our own lives and see the error of our ways, then it will be difficult to change and inform others. We must confess the areas of selfishness, sensuality, and passiveness that are destroying our lives! You can begin by discussing the Christian mind with your friends and challenging each other to aspire to greater depths of thinking. Help keep the problem in front of people.

BE DIFFERENT

At some point, we must make a decision to be different no matter the cost. When Daniel was being given food he knew would defile his body, he resolved not to eat it (see Daniel 1:8). This is a defining time in your life. Will you go with the flow of empty selves, or will you be willing to stand against the empty culture of society and church?

Choosing to change direction in the crowd could require periods of loneliness and misunderstanding. But we knew that when we chose to pick up our cross to follow Jesus (see Matthew 10:37-39). It may be hard to discipline your mind when others are out living it up. I

(Mark) remember making a decision not to date for a period of time in my life because it was too distracting and there were other areas of my life that needed focused attention. In some ways, my choice was a drag (temptation always seems to come along when we make a choice like this). But in other ways, my choice helped me grow significantly in those other areas. Are you willing to put selfish desires aside to develop your mind?

CHANGE OUR ROUTINES

For one week, note two things on a sheet of paper. First, how is your energy level? When are the peaks, and when are the valleys? How many are there of each? For me (Mark), the morning has been a low point of energy. I am at my best in the evening.

Second, what do you typically do after school, work, or dinner? When our energy is low, we often revert to passive mode and turn on the television. But the intellectual life is easier to pursue when we limit television viewing and spend more time exercising. The mind requires blood and oxygen—it needs physical activity. We're not necessarily talking about getting a personal trainer, but take a walk around the block, do a few exercises, or try some simple stretching. Different foods affect our energy levels, too. Watch your own diet to determine how foods affect you. You may need to do some research to learn what types of food keep you alert and what foods encourage passivity.

The goal with this solution to the empty self is to take advantage of low-energy times in your day by avoiding the lure of passive activity. When your energy is low, take that walk and then sit down and read a book. You'll soon find you have created better habits for those periods of time that were previously useless or detrimental to the development of your mind.

Develop Patience and Endurance

Learn how to suffer and develop patient endurance. A life of intellectual cultivation takes effort. It can even be painful. The mind, like a muscle, needs to be challenged to gain strength.

Reading books that are a little over our heads is a great way to challenge our minds to higher levels. Also, it takes time to work through important topics with sufficient care and attention. Before you think, *Oh yeah, right! I'm going to pursue intellectual suffering,* let me remind you of how much suffering you're probably already exposed to. If you're an athlete (or even just someone who gets regular exercise), you suffer in practice and during competition because you want to excel. If you are into music, you practice your instrument—a type of suffering—as you seek to master it.

We need to take a long-term perspective toward reading and study. Such a perspective will require endurance for us to stay put in a chair, make notes, and finish the book we started! If you are fidgety, you will need to learn to fight the urge and get control of yourself. Gaining control will require self-denial, suffering, and perseverance.

The best way to develop these traits is to practice the spiritual disciplines of solitude and fasting. Through solitude we learn to be alone, silent, and focused. Through fasting we learn to fight bodily distractions and our desire for instant gratification.

Develop Good Vocabulary

Keep a dictionary handy and get in the habit of looking up words you don't know. Cultivating a strong vocabulary is an important tool for a mature Christian mind. The ubiquitous and egregious (look them up!) avoidance of the dictionary today is no help to people who want to love God with all their minds. Once you discover the meaning of a new word, be sure to practice using it correctly until you are comfortable with it.

Set Intellectual Goals

Many studies have found setting and writing specific goals significantly increases our chances of meeting those goals. So, if we set some study goals for the coming year, break those into monthly and weekly goals, and put it all on paper, we're already well on our way to meeting our goals. One word of warning: We must be careful to avoid unreasonable goals, such as "Read 365 books in a year" or "Win the lottery."

But if we want to read the entire Bible (which is a reasonable goal), for instance, we need to figure out how to do that in one year. What will we have to read each month, week, and day to accomplish the goal? What resources, if any, are already out there to help us accomplish this goal?

Also, accountability to other people helps us meet our goals. Perhaps we start a study group to explore philosophy, modern art, or a theological subject. We need to find a plan that works and do it!

SMART THINKING

Evaluate how much empty self abides in your own life. Rate the empty-self characteristics listed below on a scale from 1 to 10, 1 meaning *not in my life* and 10 meaning *entrenched in my life*. (If you can't remember the details of each characteristic, review the applicable portion of the chapter.)

_____ Looks Out for Number One

_____ Childish

_____ Self-Absorbed

_____ Couch Potato

_____ Sensual

_____ Does Not Look Inward

_____ Busy

For those qualities you rated with a 5 or higher, write the reasons you think these characteristics play a big part in your life. Then spend some time in prayer, asking the Holy Spirit to convict you in these areas and show you how to combat them. Finally, take the one you rated the highest, write down two or three specific ways you plan to change it, and start today.

Part II

APPLYING
OUR
SMARTS

CHAPTER FIVE

FACILITATE THE DEBATE

USING LOGIC TO PERSUADE

[Christ] wants a child's heart, but a grown-up's head.

C. S. LEWIS

The ability to spot faulty arguments and avoid making them yourself is just one important aspect of developing healthy mental habits. During the days of the apostle Paul, rhetoricians would spin various arguments in competition (sometimes for money) to sway crowds into believing their opinions. Often these masters of persuasion would use logical fallacies to move the crowds. Today, advertisers, politicians, and religious leaders of every variety often rely on similar fallacies rather than truth and reason to get their points across.

As we explore misleading logic, we'd like you to keep a couple things in mind. First, logic is a tool for preserving the truth. If you begin with true beliefs, logic should help you draw true conclusions. Logic by itself doesn't generate true beliefs; it is merely a way of evaluating arguments to determine whether or not they are valid. Second, as with the subject of pride we touched on in chapter 4, using our superior skills with knowledge as a battering ram to win an argument is neither loving nor conducive to our relationship with the person on the other side.

PRINCIPLES OF LOGIC

We need some basic logic before we can figure out faulty logic, so we're going to look at three common syllogisms (statements in an argument that contain premises and conclusions) that can hide subtly in a person's reasoning. These syllogisms can be valid (rational) or faulty (irrational).

Keep in mind that a logical argument is different from being argumentative, which is a character flaw. The Bible tells us that it's okay to argue (debate) but not okay to be argumentative (see 1 Peter 3:15). Arguments come in two types: deductive and inductive.

DEDUCTIVE ARGUMENTS

In a deductive argument, if the premises are true, then the conclusion *must* be true. For example:

Premise 1: All Christians are idiots.
Premise 2: Billy is a Christian.
Conclusion: Billy is an idiot.

A valid argument is one in which the conclusion *must* be true *if the premises are true.* So, while this deductive argument is valid, we must ask, *Are all Christians idiots? Is Billy really a Christian?* If either of those premises is false, then the conclusion doesn't have to be true. So, logic helps us identify valid or invalid arguments, but it cannot identify whether the conclusions or premises are true or false.

Premise 1: All students attend school.
Premise 2: Billy is a student.
Conclusion: Billy attends school.

This is a valid deductive argument, and the conclusion must be true if the premises are true. The argument is also considered sound because it has true premises and thus a true conclusion.

Premise 1: All girls are human.
Premise 2: All boys are human.
Conclusion: All girls are boys.

This deductive argument is invalid because it contains true premises but an untrue conclusion.

INDUCTIVE ARGUMENTS

When we have an inductive argument, the premises merely provide support or grounds for the truth of its conclusion. It would be possible to have a valid inductive argument with true premises and a false conclusion. Consider this argument:

Premise 1: 95% of students attend school.
Premise 2: Billy is a student.
Conclusion: Billy attends school.

While the above premises are true, the first is a probability that cannot allow us to make a certain conclusion. We can, however, make a conclusion that is most likely.

SPOTTING WEAK ARGUMENTS

There is much to learn about logic (people have devoted their lives to its study), but armed with these basics, we can at least understand the following fallacies (poor arguments) that people use to argue. When you spot people using these fallacies, we suggest you don't call them on it. (Don't say, "That's preposterous! You just used a slippery slope fallacy to make your point!") Instead, use what you know about the fallacy to respond to their arguments intelligently. Let's take a look at some informal logical fallacies and the defensive moves to confront them.

The False Dilemma

This dilemma occurs when (typically) only two choices are presented when additional options may exist. People who view things as black or white tend to make this fallacy.

I (Mark) remember being a teenager and wanting to start listening to Christian rock music. My parents were strongly against it. They thought, *Bad people listen to rock music and good people don't.* The two ideas in that statement were reality to them, but were they true? Rather than slamming my bedroom door and wasting time being angry at my parents, I appealed to them with reason. When things had calmed, I asked my dad if I could make an appeal. (Regardless of the fallacy in their statement, I had to honor my parents and obey them, a non-negotiable.) The problem with my parents' fallacy is that it took attention away from the real issue, a third position they hadn't considered: "There are good people who listen to Christian rock music."

Defensive Move: I explained the third position to them and supported my claim with evidence: I mentioned a Christian teenager they knew and respected who listened to rock music and who was also a responsible, good kid. After I calmly explained the third option and supported my argument intelligently, my parents agreed to let me listen to rock music that met their approval.

Ignorance

This fallacy states that because something has not been proven to be true, it must be false. The opposite is also a fallacy: If something hasn't been proven false, it must be true.

I have a friend who is into natural remedies for illness. (She takes herbs and stuff like that when she is sick.) I asked her if it was wise to put things into her body when she knows very little about them. She argued, "Science hasn't proven that these herbs are harmful, so they probably aren't."

Defensive Move: When someone presents a fallacy of ignorance, we need to identify her premise and point out that just because the premise lacks proof does not mean we can correctly draw a certain conclusion.

Slippery Slope

When a premise is followed by a series of increasingly unreasonable consequences, we call this a slippery slope argument.

We know of a certain "dry" city, meaning a person cannot bring alcoholic beverages inside the city limits. Recently, citizens had an opportunity to vote on the matter of whether alcohol should or should not be allowed in the city. The people opposed to having alcohol in the city distributed flyers making their case. They said that if residents allowed alcohol into the city, their neighborhoods would attract less desirable inhabitants, and eventually adult sex shops and strip clubs would open as well.

This group had some strong arguments, but these particular ones actually were quite weak. The group made a slippery slope argument that if "A" happened, then "B", "C", and "D" were sure to follow. There is little to no evidence to support those results. The group had stronger, more reasonable, and less fallacious arguments they could have used, but they went with the slippery slope (and won, we might add!).

Defensive Move: Identify the "if" premise (in this case *if we let alcohol into the city)* and the final result *(strip clubs would open)* and then explain that the final result need not occur just because of the initial premise. For example, other cities allow alcohol and have never had a strip club open.

Attacking the Person (Ad Hominem)

An ad hominem attack occurs when the credibility of the arguer is questioned rather than the merits of her arguments.

One day in my political science class in high school, I (Mark) was arguing the morality of abortion (taking a pro-life position). The person I was debating stood up and said, "Well, of course you would have that opinion. You are a man and can't even get pregnant!" Obviously, my gender has nothing to do with whether abortion is right or wrong.

Now, in some courtroom television dramas, you will see lawyers personally attack the credibility and character of their witnesses. This is not an ad hominem argument. The difference is that with an ad hominem attack, the focus of the argument shifts to the arguer. In a courtroom, on the other hand, the argument does not (or should not) shift to attack the witness; the argument is focused on what the witness says to determine the credibility and trustworthiness of her testimony.

Defensive Move: An attack on the person distracts from the main points of the argument. To defend or expose this argument, you must show that the personal attack has no bearing on the validity of the argument and is a distraction from the central argument. In my polisci class, I had to reason that the arguer's gender has no bearing on the argument: whether an unborn fetus is life or not.

Style over Substance

This type of fallacy gives more weight to the style of the arguer rather than the argument itself. In a famous presidential debate between Richard Nixon and John F. Kennedy, radio listeners believed Nixon was the winner based on the arguments he had made, whereas television viewers declared JFK the winner. The difference was that JFK's appearance was more appealing than Nixon's (Nixon was ill and sweating profusely, which made him appear weak). Those who watched these debates on television were impacted by the style over the substance of each man's campaign.

From salespeople to ministers, people will often fill their presentations with style to woo you to their side, sometimes without offering valid arguments. Be on guard!

Defensive Move: This one is difficult to defend because our presentation naturally influences people in ways that are difficult to discern and expose. It's best to have a good argument and present it as attractively as possible. Also keep this knowledge in mind when observing others who are trying to influence you. Are you giving more credibility to their style or to the actual substance of their argument?

Begging the Question

Begging the question occurs when a premise can be believed only by already believing the conclusion. This can happen when we state the conclusion in a different manner than the premise. For instance, if you were to argue for God's existence this way, you would be begging the question: "We know God exists because the Bible says so, and we know the Bible is true because it is God's Word and God never lies." The conclusion that God exists is true, but the argument that supports it begs the question. It does so because the argument assumes the Bible is true because God (whose existence we are arguing for) says so.

Darrell Bock, a professor at Dallas Theological Seminary, wrote a book called *Breaking the Da Vinci Code.*[17] Dan Brown's novel *The Da Vinci Code*[18] cast some serious doubt regarding the reliability of Scripture and the person and nature of Christ. Because Brown brought the authority of Scripture into question, it was impossible for Bock to argue for the character of Christ through using the Bible without begging the question. Christians would buy the argument, but nonbelievers would not. So in Bock's book, he had to form his arguments in such a way as to avoid begging the question and weakening his arguments.

Defensive Move: When someone "begs the question," show him that in order to believe the premise you must already believe the conclusion is true. This gets Christians into trouble because we often use the Bible as our sole source of evidence for our conclusion.

Irrelevant Conclusion

Irrelevant conclusions occur when a person is trying to prove one thing and ends up with a conclusion their argument doesn't necessarily support. For example, the AIDS crisis in Africa is a monumental world issue; some countries estimate that nearly half of Africa's citizens are infected. Most people would agree that we need to take action, but many of the arguments for doing so make irrelevant conclusions.

We've heard one person say, "We need to distribute more condoms to the African people and have them readily available. People are dying in record numbers and children are being orphaned because their parents have died as a result of AIDS. You can't deny that this crisis will impact future generations." This argument discusses the impact of AIDS on the culture, but it does not support the notion that distributing condoms will be effective.

Defensive Move: Notice that the argument for condom distribution to help the AIDS crisis concluded with some of the impact of the epidemic but did not support that condoms could help. To defend an irrelevant conclusion fallacy, you must show that the conclusion is not supported by the argument. In the AIDS case, the argument supports the conclusion that the AIDS crisis needs our attention but doesn't give evidence that condom distribution is the most effective (or even helpful) solution.

Straw Man

A man made out of straw (like a scarecrow) is an easy thing to defeat because he is not real (and is therefore less complex). People often create a "straw man" when arguing their point against the opposition because the "straw man" is easier to defeat. Basically, the one making an argument describes his opponent's position with the weakest arguments, or the one making the argument completely creates the opposition's position based on his own ideas. This is an important fallacy to understand because those opposed to Christianity often argue against a "Christian straw man." And we as Christians also create straw men for those who oppose us.

Consider the debate between creation and evolution. Both sides have created straw men of their opponents, and few even hear what the other side is saying. A scientist might say, "Creationists are unreasonable because they believe that the world began in 4004 BC and that Noah had every species of animal that we have today in the ark with him at the Flood. Creationist science is not science at all but merely myth. Their claims are hypotheses without any scientific exploration of the truth."

Now, very few creationists hold that earth began in 4004 BC (that was a claim one man made and many believed until the idea failed to pass higher scrutiny). However, in its infancy, creationist thinking did try to explain science by postulating nonscientific ideas about how science did not refute God's creation of the world—such as saying the earth might appear older because God created everything with the appearance of age. Creationists today are using science now to support their claims. So the scientist makes a creationist straw man that can be easily defeated—one whose ideas are not the strongest arguments that could be made for his case.

But the church creates straw men, too, especially of its enemies. We create straw men opponents for our attacks against evolutionists, Hollywood, political parties, other religions, and so on. I (Mark) remember going to a seminar when I was young to hear an "expert" on Mormonism teach us why Mormons were not Christians and how to argue against their faith. I left confident I could do that. Well, my first encounter with a Mormon quickly revealed that the arguments I'd learned were straw man arguments. This Mormon actually told me I had some severe misunderstandings about Mormonism. Sure enough, later study and interaction with other Mormons confirmed that this "expert" had sold us a weak and inaccurate portrayal of Mormon beliefs and practices.

Creating weak opponents is easy, unfortunately. The less we interact with nonbelievers, the more we grow to believe in the superiority of Christian arguments because they are rarely tested with anyone except those who reinforce our beliefs.

Defensive Move: To defeat a straw man argument, you must show that your position actually has stronger arguments than are being presented by the opposition. Reliable data must also be used to counter "the straw man."

Red Herring

The name of this fallacy has an interesting background. When training hunting dogs, a red herring (a fish) would be used to confuse the dogs to follow that scent rather than the scent of the animal they were tracking. Well-trained dogs would not lose the original scent they were tracking. So the red herring is an argument that diverts the course of the discussion to other topics.

Recently there has been a lot of press about legalizing gay marriages. I have seen a number of Christians get involved in red herring fallacies when arguing their position on gay marriage. Typically, after realizing the weakness of their arguments, the Christian starts going in another direction. For example: "Marriage must remain defined as between a man and a woman and not between members of the same sex. This is just another tactic of the gay community to promote their gay agenda. They want to be accepted by society so they can convert our children to homosexuality." The topic, whether marriage should remain defined as a union between a man and a woman, was never really addressed after the proposition was made! Instead, the Christian attacked the gay community, which could have derailed the conversation to an emotionally charged (and possibly irrelevant) defense by the proponent of gay marriage.

Defensive Move: We need to restate and clarify what the nature of the argument is and show that our opponent is trying to lead us to other subject matter. In the gay-marriage scenario, the proponent of gay marriage successfully did this. She simply said, "There you go trying to scare everybody. I'm not trying to convert anyone to homosexuality. I believe that you are either born gay or not gay. But we are discussing whether marriage should be defined as between a man and a woman. Because marriage is a cultural expression, we as a culture can define it any way we like. I was born gay, so let me have a gay marriage." With this calm response (she won style points for not getting flustered), she refused to allow the conversation to go off-topic and avoided a shouting match. She effectively used what the Christian said to strengthen her argument for the gay marriage, while the Christian wasted an opportunity.

Genetic Fallacy

The genetic fallacy refers to the origin of an idea as a means to accept or reject it. An example of the genetic fallacy would be to argue, "The origin of God came from man's inability to cope with fear and make sense of the universe around him. Scared, confused man created God. So it is not reasonable to believe in God." This is not how the idea of God originated, but if we were to assume it were, the assumption would be utterly irrelevant in judging whether or not one should believe in God.

At the beginning of this book, we shared an e-mail from Randee, who was struggling to know whether she was a Christian only because she was raised in a Christian home. Someone had made this argument to her: "You are a Christian because you were raised in a Christian home. If you had been raised in a Hindu home, you would be a Hindu. Therefore, it doesn't really matter whether you are a Christian or a Hindu." This argument is a genetic fallacy. While it is true that the home a person grows up in will influence that person's faith, the origin of that faith has nothing to do with its validity. The sociology and psychology of this question bring up interesting points, but those would be relevant to a separate investigation.

The genetic fallacy reminds us of grade school when a teacher would ask a student, "Why did you throw the rock at the window?" and the response would be, "Because David told me to." The teacher would then ask, "So if David told you to jump off a bridge, would you do that, too?" The teacher's question just exposed a genetic fallacy. Just because a certain person held to or originated an idea doesn't mean it's valid. Motives are one thing; rational grounds and evidence are another.

Defensive Move: To defeat the genetic fallacy, you must expose the origin of the idea as separate from whether that idea is true.

Fallacies of Emotion

Emotional manipulation is something we all hope to avoid, whether we are being manipulated or doing the manipulating. Within the church and without (in fact, within loads of places in society), emotions are often a ploy of fallacious thinking. We must learn to identify emotion and separate it from reasonable arguments if we are going to represent the truth of Christ in this world. This is not to say that emotions are bad, but they must be balanced with good reasoning.

Defensive Move: Keeping our emotions in check regarding beliefs

that are dear to us is difficult. Practice self-control and learn to iden-\
tify when someone is pushing your buttons.

Appeal to People

Accepting a belief as true because it is widely held or believed by \
a certain sector of the population is called an appeal to "popular-\
ity" (argumentum ad populum). Before Columbus provided strong
evidence that the world was indeed round, most people believed that
the world was flat. But just because this was believed by a majority did
not have any bearing on whether the belief was true or false. Here is
an example: "The majority of Americans do not believe that abortion
is murder, so you should get with the times and drop your antiquated
view that life begins at conception." Just because the majority believes
that abortion is not murder doesn't make that belief true.

In the United States, we support democracy—in other words, we
believe that everyone should have a voice. When many people agree
on a belief, their numbers can make them powerful. Falling prey to
this type of fallacy can happen because we subconsciously think, *Well,
if that many people believe something, then it must be true.* But majority
opinion and numbers do not guarantee truth.

Another example of this fallacy is to align an idea with an elite
group to try to make the concept valid. For instance, "No civilized
human being could ever approve of the barbaric use of war in modern
times. We have peaceful means of engaging those we are in conflict
with, and any educated, cultured person would never accept war as an
acceptable solution to a problem." This argument gives the impres-
sion that if we do not agree, we are simpletons and only sophisticated
people have figured out the truth.

Consider this similar argument: "Only close-minded people could
possibly accept the claims of Christianity. Educated, open-minded
people realize that there are no absolute truths, so you Christians

should stop claiming that Christ is the only way to God." Here the argument requires the hearer to accept the beliefs of the more "elite" group, but the argument includes no real evidence to believe one way or the other.

Defensive Move: Point out that just because a certain group or large number of people believe something doesn't make it true.

Appeal to Force

In an appeal to force, the person making the argument describes unpleasant consequences that will result if we do not agree. Imagine a church youth group that says, "Drinking alcohol is wrong, and if you drink, we will no longer consider you a friend." Have you been to a church like this? Can you see why this is a weak argument? While we are certain that this group would cease to associate with us if they caught us drinking alcohol, they have not given a reasoned argument for why drinking is wrong. All they have done is made an ultimatum and bullied us into accepting it.

Unfortunately, within a community, this fallacy can be used to manipulate many people's beliefs. How about this one: "Jesus is the only way to God. If you don't trust that Jesus died for your sins, you will experience great suffering in hell." Yes, this is an appeal to force. Even though the claim (Jesus is the only way to God) is true, support for that claim is not made through revealing the consequences of not believing.

Defensive Move: To expose this fallacy, you must show that the threat (we will no longer be your friend) has nothing to do with the truth or falsity of the proposition (drinking alcohol is wrong).

Appeal to Pity

Someone making an appeal to pity will use psychologically moving arguments that are logically irrelevant to support their premise.

At the time of this writing, there is a nationwide debate about the morality of embryonic stem cell research. Simply stated, many people do not advocate the use of human embryos for scientific experiments on the grounds that it is morally wrong, while others advocate the use because they feel it is morally right to serve the greater good.

This issue is ripe (on both sides of the argument) for an appeal to pity. Those who are in favor of the research have used spokespeople such as the late Christopher Reeve (the popular actor who was paralyzed after an injury involving a horse) to make their case. While many times Mr. Reeve offered arguments for stem cell research, others have referenced his condition as means to evoke pity, such as, "If you don't support embryonic stem cell research, you are condemning wonderful people like Christopher Reeve to a wheelchair." This argument has nothing to do with the serious ethical issues surrounding this research.

The appeal to pity is a powerful influencer, and we use it all the time knowingly and unknowingly. We've shared a "big issue" use of the fallacy, but here is one that is more common: "I hope you like my final semester project. I stayed up the last several nights to complete it and missed an important football game." If the person is lucky, this plea might get him a better grade, but the amount of time he spent on the project and the sacrifices he made have nothing to do with the content or quality of the work.

People use the appeal to pity for two reasons. First, they are trying to influence people to believe something, and using pity is an effective way to do so. Second, they are trying to help people who are in need, but they are not finding the best methods. With the stem cell research issue, for example, they may use the plight of Christopher Reeve to influence others to their position. If, on the other hand, they are trying to help people like Christopher Reeve, there may be better ways than federally funding stem cell research to do that.

Defensive Move: To expose an appeal to pity, we must reveal that the claim (stem cell research should be federally funded) has nothing to do with the pitiful circumstance (a nice guy was condemned to a wheelchair and eventually died). But when we do this, it is important not to be or appear cold or callous. As Christians, we are to be loving people who use our minds. Arguing against this kind of fallacy can easily make us appear compassionless.

As Christians, we must learn to be compassionate with both our hearts and our minds. Exposing the fallacy of the argument may be easy, but using our minds to discover the best way to help others in need may not be so easy.

CLOSING ARGUMENTS

Though we haven't listed every possible fallacy, we've uncovered some of those you are likely to make or have used on you. Remember that a claim can be true even if it's presented with a fallacious argument. What we mean is that focusing solely on the methods of an argument can be just as dangerous as focusing solely on the subject of the argument.

Remember, too, that a person using a fallacy is probably not being intentionally deceptive or manipulative. We all have made fallacious arguments with the best of intentions, so rather than get in the face of those whose arguments are weak, let's help them spot the weaknesses of reasoned arguments with care and concern.

Keep in mind that in debating, we are seeking truth.

SMART THINKING

During the next week, watch for the fallacies described in this chapter and write down any you notice. You might hear them from friends or teachers, or you might come across them on television or in a magazine or newspaper. Take one fallacy you hear, write it down, and then, using the examples in this chapter to help you, write why the argument doesn't work.

CHAPTER SIX

NOT SCARED TO SHARE ANYMORE

EVANGELIZING WITH BRAINS

So [Paul] reasoned in the synagogue with the Jews and the God-fearing Greeks, as well as in the marketplace day by day with those who happened to be there.

ACTS 17:17

For many of us, the idea of sharing our faith with another person is intimidating at best. We convince ourselves that we are inadequate to share or that we are not mature enough in the faith to be good witnesses for the good news that Jesus offers to a lost world. We have developed all kinds of strategies, programs, and gimmicks for making the sharing of our faith more palatable. But, honestly, most of us are just scared to share.

Not only are we scared to share but when we do share, we don't have all the facts. Recent Barna research reports that two-thirds of Christian teenagers had shared their faith at least once in the year prior to the survey. That was encouraging to hear. But the report quickly turned discouraging. When the evangelizers were asked about their basic beliefs, one out of five believed that Jesus had sinned on earth; one out of four believed that the Holy Spirit wasn't real; one in three said the Devil did not exist; and one out of two believed that two people could have conflicting beliefs and both be right.[19] Whoa! Just what were they sharing?

As we've explored in this book, our fear comes from a lack of intellectual development regarding our faith in Christ. Worse, when we share our faith and we are uninformed and not prepared, our lack of accurate information about Christianity may actually lead others astray.

People with good intentions unfortunately have taught us methods for ineffective and sometimes downright embarrassing evangelism—the kind we need to stop attempting. Instead, we can sharpen our smarts and partner with the Holy Spirit for powerful evangelism. Again, our effectiveness for the kingdom of God depends a whole lot on our minds. We'll show you here ways we've abandoned our intellect in evangelism and—you guessed it—ways to bring it back into the mix.

GO MAKE DISCIPLES

Why must we evangelize? Because Jesus commanded it. Before He left the earth, He gave His disciples the Great Commission: "Therefore go and make disciples of all nations, baptizing them in the name of the Father, and of the Son and of the Holy Spirit, and teaching them to obey everything I have commanded you" (Matthew 28:19,20). To the church's credit, we have always sought to fulfill this great mission at home and abroad, but, unfortunately we have distorted or misunderstood many of the basics of this command.

First, we focus too much on making converts—getting people to "pray the prayer," "walk the walk," or say they "have Jesus in their heart." We may get converts, but how long do they remain so when we leave the mind out of the process? The call of Christ is actually to *make disciples,* which goes far beyond that initial acceptance of Christ.

Despite the gimmicks out there, the church has had some success in training believers how to share their faith. But the church has rarely trained believers how to make disciples. Making disciples means helping others become true followers of Christ. That takes time and commitment. No one becomes a truly devoted follower without having solid reasons for doing so.

HOW NOT TO MAKE A DISCIPLE

So, we need to make disciples, and we need intellectual support to do so. Here are some methods of evangelism we want to avoid.

EMOTIONAL VERSUS REASONED

As we touched on in earlier chapters, most of us don't know how to present step-by-step evidence that supports our conclusions for trusting in Christ for one's salvation. As a result, Christians have resorted to emotional ploys and sales pitches aimed at explaining the benefits of Christianity to the unbeliever.

Many people have an emotional experience when coming to faith in Christ, and that's okay. But we often wrongly manipulate that to make converts. We (and the person we evangelize) must be able to give a reasoned case for why we believe, per 1 Peter 3:15. And it is only through unbelievers' reasonable understanding of what Christ has done for them that we can be convinced they truly do believe.

ONE-SIZE-FITS-ALL VERSUS CUSTOM-FIT

Countless acrostics (each letter in a word is the first letter of another word) and alliterations (every word for something begins with the same letter) have been formed to help us present the gospel. These and similar systems are designed to make the gospel easier to remember and share, but how difficult can it be to remember the most important truth we can know in life?

Systems like these dumb down the simple yet deeply profound message, making God's truth seem weak, corny, and foolish. Using a canned strategy to say, "God loves you and has a wonderful plan for your life," contradicts the very message it is delivering. The formulaic approach lacks sincerity and credibility because we're trying to apply it to unique creations of God.

TOOL VERSUS TOOLBOX

People slap all kinds of labels on the methods they use in order to shy away from sharing their faith. I've heard people say that you have to feed people before they can hear the message, yet Jesus said, "Don't worry about what you will eat or drink, but seek first the kingdom of God and his righteousness" (see Matthew 6:31-33). Other people claim they are friendship evangelists—that they will allow their lifestyle and friendship to be the necessary witnesses—yet in Romans it says, "How will they hear unless someone shared the message?" (see Romans 10:14,15).

Providing food and using lifestyle and friendship as witnesses are not wrong facilitators to sharing our faith, and, in fact, they may be quite conducive. But if we rely on the tool rather than the toolbox, we're going down an ineffective track. In my (Mark's) thirty years of following Christ, there are only a couple of times I've ever had an unbeliever initiate a conversation about Christ. That leaves you and me with the responsibility to initiate.

CLEVER VERSUS POWERFUL

In my (Mark's) days as a magician, I would be asked to come and share the gospel message. I felt uncomfortable using a magic trick as my illustration. The use of deception to illustrate the most incredible truth seemed disingenuous. What's more, reducing the gospel to a magic trick seemed to weaken the power of Christ's death and resurrection.

Christians continually come up with corny gimmicks (no matter how clever) to share the faith, and, well, they make Jesus corny. I'd rather be hated than considered annoying or goofy when people identify me with Christ. But human beings love novelty, and Christians are no exception. As amazing as it sounds, we actually get bored with the message of the gospel. (Boredom is definitely a sign we aren't using our minds to explore the profound mysteries of our faith!)

One time when doing a magic show for a church, I ended my thirty minutes of magic and spent the next thirty minutes sharing a reasoned case for Christ. When it was over, I was excited to learn that many of those in attendance had come to trust in Christ for their salvation. But I also learned the pastor wasn't too happy with me; he was disappointed I didn't do more magic tricks. For him, the method of sharing outweighed the message and the mission of evangelism.

SUCCESSFUL DISCIPLEMAKING

Those weak strategies for sharing our faith are clearly not what Christ had in mind when He charged His disciples with making disciples of every nation, tribe, and language. Instead, we must stand on Christ. He is the power in the message. He *is* the message. Letting Him lead us is primary, but He expects us to live up to our responsibility with integrity. We've listed some ways to do that here.

Go!

The beginning of the Great Commission starts with the word *go*. Too often our evangelism is structured around the idea of *come*. We invite people to church, programs, and Christian events, hoping those will do the work of evangelism. While there is nothing wrong with inviting people to events, it is a weak approach.

The idea in "Go" is to seek out those who are lost and to bring the gospel to them. Then we can welcome them into the body of Christ, where they can begin growing as disciples. As we will see in chapter 10, God has given us talents and interests to "Go" and tell the message in the many different areas of our lives.

BE PREPARED TO GIVE REASONS

It is true that as we share our faith there will be some who challenge what we believe. The good news is, there are other Christians who have gone before us who can help us work through those challenges. The key to making disciples is being discipled ourselves. We need to find mature Christians to help us grow spiritually. They can help us develop good arguments for what we believe about Christ.

LISTEN FIRST

Being prepared to share is critical, but we must also cultivate a desire and ability to listen. In fact, listening is rarely talked about in most evangelism training. In order to truly respond with Christ to people, we need to know what they believe, what they understand about Christ (if anything), and what their attitude toward faith is. Having an idea where other people are coming from allows us to reason *with* them rather than ineffectually speaking *at* them. Disciplemaking is a dynamic process, not a one-way experience.

For example, I (Mark) have shared my faith with people who thought they knew about Christ and were surprised to realize they had faulty information about Him. I might have overlooked some of the correct information if I hadn't first learned what they knew. Others I've shared with were hostile toward God because of something bad that happened in their life. Until they stopped to think about and (hopefully) resolve why they were angry with God, they were unable to really hear any other information about Him. Knowing this helped me introduce the gospel via topics that were relevant to these people (such as justice and forgiveness). Still others had serious doubts about the reliability of the Bible and the historical reality of Christ. Sharing with them required yet another approach, one that included extrabiblical details in support of these truths. Regardless of where people are coming from, sharing in every case requires reason as a foundation.

And finally, letting go of the outcome is critical to our effectiveness. We can't force people to convert. We must ask the Holy Spirit to give us the right words to instigate them in bringing about their change. We need not fear the person's reaction to us — God can handle it. Assuming what questions the person will ask and what issues will come up is easy and dangerous. If the person isn't cooperating with our expectations, we damage the relationship by trying to manipulate the person, however subtly. Avoid this by doing a regular check on your expectations and reminding yourself who's really in charge.

If we truly care about others, we'll take the time to listen and know them, sharing the most important truth with them as the Holy Spirit gives us opportunity and prompts us.

BE AUTHENTIC AND VULNERABLE WHILE LEARNING

When sharing our faith, we must be prepared for all of the great questions out there that will stump us. Don't be afraid of not having an answer for every question. Our lack of answers does not mean our faith is weak or we can't be effective witnesses. In fact, trying to act as though we have all the answers can actually work against us, making us appear full of platitudes and naïveté. People don't expect us to know everything, so we can (and should) be honest.

When we encounter a question we can't answer, we can say

something like, "Wow, that's a great question from a position I haven't considered. God wouldn't want me to insult your intelligence, so would you mind if I took some time to think about my response and get back to you later?" People will appreciate this honesty far more than a pat answer.

The good news is that the more we grow in our faith (intellectually and spiritually), the less we'll find ourselves without a response. It's not that we'll have collected all the answers; it's just that we'll recognize common questions and know the prevailing ideas about them.

BE IN IT FOR THE LONG HAUL

Disciplemaking is not a fast endeavor; it requires not only encouraging a person to believe but investing into his or her life. As we share, we need to keep in mind the last portion of the Great Commission: to teach disciples all that Christ commanded.

The disciplemaking process begins when a person trusts in Christ. The apostle Paul said, "We proclaim [Christ], admonishing and teaching everyone with all wisdom, so that we may present everyone perfect in Christ. To this end I labor, struggling with all his energy, which so powerfully works in me" (1 Corinthians 1:28-29). As we develop our own faith, we must labor with people to help them develop their own, praying for them steadfastly along the entire way.

THE NEED FOR APOLOGETICS

In the next chapter, we'll expand on some of the ideas explored here by discussing apologetics, the art of defending our faith. Apologetic skills are necessary to smart evangelism.

AGAIN, GO MAKE DISCIPLES

Never be satisfied with your level of knowledge and understanding.

God's truth is deep and rich enough for a life filled with ever-expanding learning. Continue to read books that challenge your thinking, and hang out with other Christians committed to developing their intellect.

The growth of your mind will make you a powerful magnet for drawing people into the kingdom of God. Let Him use you. Go . . . !

SMART THINKING

Think of one person in your life you're not certain what he or she believes about Jesus Christ. Go to that person sometime this week and share the assignment you've been given (from this book). Your mission is to first collect a few questions the person has about Jesus and Christianity, second seek the answers, and third return and share your findings.

Once you have the questions, work with a mature Christian (maybe a parent, youth leader, or friend) and find the answers from reliable sources (the Bible, books written by trusted Christians, or extrabiblical books on subjects such as history or archaeology). Make sure you understand the answers and are comfortable with sharing them before reporting back to your friend.

After you talk about the questions and answers, ask for your friend's reaction to your findings and whether she has more questions. Be sensitive to opportunities provided by the Holy Spirit for you to ask the person whether she believes Christ died for her sin. And if your friend ultimately chooses to follow Christ, don't abandon her. Help your friend grow in Christ by studying the Bible with her and including her in church fellowship.

CHAPTER SEVEN

"GOD SAID IT. I BELIEVE IT. DOESN'T THAT SETTLE IT?"

REASONING LIKE SCHOLARS

*Western civilization is for the first time in its history in
danger of dying. The reason is spiritual. It is losing its life, its
soul; that soul was the Christian faith. . . . We do apologetics
not to save the church but to save the world.*

PETER KREEFT AND RON TACELLI

People come to faith in Christ in many ways, at different ages, and over long and short periods of time. Some might hear the truth and simply accept it. Other people might come to faith because Christ fulfills the emptiness in their life. There are others who come to faith only after seriously researching everything they can about Christianity and realizing its undeniable truth and authenticity. Regardless of the basic reasons you believe, you can believe with greater faith when you learn the details supporting it. Some have argued that they don't need any proof to believe. There's nothing necessarily wrong with that. But to grow intellectually and deepen our faith, we must be able to defend what we claim to be true. That's where apologetics comes in.

Christian apologetics can be defined as that New Testament ministry that seeks to provide rational grounds for believing Christianity and to respond to objections raised against Christianity. So apologetics is a ministry designed to help unbelievers overcome intellectual obstacles to conversion and remove doubts that hinder their spiritual growth. Understanding and using apologetics is necessary for developing our minds.

When I (Mark) was a teenager, I had several pink stickers attached to my stuff (I do wish they had not been pink!) that said, *God Said It! I Believe It! That Settles It!* I felt bold and strong in my beliefs for sporting such a statement on all of my books, on my locker, and in my bedroom. The only problem was, my faith rarely felt settled. When others challenged me about what I believed, I would become paralyzed with the inability to speak (anyone who knows me will find that difficult to imagine).

Jude 3 admonishes us to "contend earnestly" (NASB) for the faith, which implies engaging in a contest, struggle, conflict, or debate by the pious in the heroic struggle for religious truth, justice, and virtue. We see examples of the struggle throughout Scripture. In Acts, Paul argued, reasoned, presented evidence, and tried rationally to persuade others to become Christians (Acts 14:15-17; 17:2-4,16-31; 18:4; 19:8-9). He brought to center stage the truth and reasonableness of the gospel, not the fact that it addresses any "needs" of the moment. Though the benefits of believing are important, the fact that the gospel is true and reasonable takes precedence. Christ regularly engaged in logical debate and rational argument to challenge false, destructive ideologies in His culture. On several occasions, He encouraged people to believe Him by not only His words but also the evidence of His miracles.

In this way, Jesus and Paul were continuing a style of persuasion used by prophets throughout the Old Testament. On a regular basis, prophets appealed to evidence to justify belief in the biblical God or in the divine authority of their inspired message. The evidence they used included fulfilled prophecy, the historical fact of miracles, and the impossibility of finite pagan deities being the cause of such a well-ordered universe. The prophets did not say, "God Said It! I Believe It! That Settles It!"

To explain the methods of apologetic reasoning employed by the prophets, Paul, and Jesus, we've included in this chapter examples of contending with three types of objections Christians typically face: skepticism, scientism, and moral relativism. These three philosophies underlie many people's belief systems, whether they know it or not, and we need to learn to recognize them when they show up in arguments about moral or spiritual issues. Know these positions and then you will be able to refute them, whether subtly or directly.

Try not to be intimidated if some of these arguments seem challenging to identify and articulate. You may even need to read the segments several times until they click. In any case, no one person alone is up to accomplishing the art of apologetics. We need to be working in community with other believers to strengthen and further develop our apologetic skills.

ANSWERING SKEPTICISM

If you have been a Christian for a while, you no doubt have been engaged at one time or another in a seemingly endless argument with a skeptic. These people get a kick out of spending concentrated time playing with Christian thoughts and emotions (usually the emotions).

Along with knowing our stuff, a little self-control will go a long way in building our credibility with another person. We can avoid fueling the skeptic (or any other aggressor) by refusing to show frustration when she backs us into a corner. We need to remain calm and polite and take a moment to think. If we end up stumped, we can tell her we would like more time to consider her arguments and then get back with her.

A conversation with a skeptic might look like this:

You: Jesus said He is the way, the truth, and the life — that no one can access God without believing in Christ.

Them: Oh, yeah? Says who?

You: Jesus said so. It is in the Bible.

Them: How do you know the Bible, or Jesus for that matter, can be trusted?

You: Well, Jesus was the Son of God.

Them: How do you know that?

You: The Bible tells me so.

Them: Why do you trust the Bible?

You: It is God's Word. God's Word is truth!

Them: Really? How do you know that?

There are many forms of skeptics, but for now we'll define a skeptic as someone who does not believe that people have knowledge or rationally held beliefs. Some skeptics are "global" skeptics. They hold their skepticism about all beliefs. Others are "local" skeptics. They may allow for knowledge in certain areas, such as science or mathematics, while confining their skepticism to, say, ethical or religious claims. To refute skepticism, we need to learn about what's called *the problem of criterion*.[20]

THE PROBLEM OF CRITERION

How do we determine what is knowledge and what is not? This is the problem of criterion, and it involves two primary questions. First, *What is it that we know?* (In other words, *What specific items of knowledge do we possess?* and *What is the extent or limit of that knowledge?*) Second, *How do we decide the criteria to determine whether we know something?* (In other words, *What can be used to evaluate whether something can be considered knowledge?*)

For example, if we wanted to sort all our beliefs into two groups—the true or justified ones, and the false or unjustified ones—we would need to answer at least one of the questions. And here is where the problem of criterion becomes obvious: Before we can answer the first question, *What is it that I know?* we must answer the second question, *How can I know something?* Yet before we can answer the second question, we must answer the first.

If we don't know how we know things, how can we know anything at all? But if we don't know some things before we ask how we can know things, we have nothing we can base answers on. Does your brain hurt yet?

There are three ways people have resorted to dealing with this problem.

Skepticism

The *skeptic* claims that no good solution to the problem exists and thus there is no knowledge. The next two solutions are advocated by those who claim we do have knowledge.

Methodism

Methodism (not the denomination), advocated by philosophers John Locke and René Descartes, begins with a criterion for what does and does not count as knowledge. In other words, we start with the answer to question two and then discover the answer to question one. The criterion is developed first. For instance, before we can know there is a tree in the yard, we must meet a certain criterion that is suitable for knowing matter exists. Let's say that criterion is as follows: If something can be tested with our five senses, then it can be an item of knowledge. Thus, if we can sense the tree through touch, taste, sight, and smell, we can know the tree exists.

The problem with Methodism is that the argument for the criterion can be similar to holding a mirror up to a mirror; an infinity of arguments must be made to defend the criteria. For instance, John Locke and René Descartes developed very different criteria for establishing what could be considered an item of knowledge. For a person to defend his criterion, he must argue the criterion for that, which then must be argued, and then that argument argued, and we can see this could go on forever. In this way, Methodism essentially defeats itself.

Particularism

Particularism was advocated by such philosophers as Thomas Reid, Roderick Chisholm, and G. E. Moore. According to the particularists, we start by knowing specific, clear items of knowledge. For example, we had toast for breakfast, there is a tree in front of us or perhaps that we seem to see a tree, that 7+5=12, that mercy is a virtue, and so on. Basically, we can know some things directly without needing criteria to know how we know them or even that we know them. We know many things without being able to prove that we do or without fully understanding them. We simply identify clear instances of knowing without having to possess or apply any criteria for knowledge. We may then at some time reflect on these instances and go on to develop criteria for knowledge that is consistent with them.

THE SKEPTIC ATTACKS THE PARTICULARIST

There are two objections the skeptic can raise against the particularist. First, the particularist simply assumes his answer to whether we have knowledge. The skeptic wants to know how the particularist knows we have this knowledge. Isn't it possible that the particularist is wrong and only "thinks" he has this knowledge?

Skeptic: So you claim there is knowledge that you just *know*?

Particular man: Yes, I know things without having to prove that I know them or that they are, in fact, knowledge.

Skeptic: How do you know this knowledge? Isn't it possible that you are wrong and only "think" you have knowledge?

Particular man: Okay, then. What is the reason for your skepticism? All you ask is, "How do you know?" but you never offer any argument for a serious objection to knowledge.

Skeptic: In order for me to argue against knowledge, I would have to have something to measure knowledge, and no one can know that.

Particular man: Exactly! If we did not have some knowledge about some things, we could not "doubt" anything. You cannot rationally assert your skepticism because it cannot be asserted without having some self-evident knowledge. You'd have to be a particularist to get to your point!

The second attack comes when the skeptic attempts to force the particularist into Methodism.

Skeptic: Okay, then. How do you know?

(The skeptic knows he can refute the methodist, so the particularist must stay away from this trap.)

Particular man: I believe I can know some things without having to claim why I know this. For instance, I know that lying is wrong, even if I don't know how it is that I know this. But, Mr. Skeptic, why do you think that I have to know how I know this before I can know it?

Skeptic: Hmmm. But isn't it a logical possibility that you are wrong?

Particular man: Just because it's logically possible I am wrong in a specific instance of knowledge does not mean that I am mistaken or that you have any good reason to believe that I am wrong. Until you can provide a good reason for thinking my instances of knowledge fail, the mere logical possibility that I am wrong will not suffice.

Skeptic: So, tell me something you believe to be true.

Particular man: I went to Disneyland several days ago.

Skeptic: Isn't it possible that you were born five seconds ago with a memory and that your memory is deceiving you?

Particular man: Just because the statement "Particular Man was born five seconds ago with a memory" is not a logical contradiction and could be true as a bare logical possibility does not mean we have good reason to believe it is correct.

Skeptic: But it is possible!

Particular man: Sure, but unless you provide good reasons to believe that to be the case, the simple possibility of it being true is not sufficient to question my trip to Disneyland.

The skeptic and the particularist tend to approach knowledge quite differently. For the *skeptic*, the burden of proof is on the one claiming to know something. If one can logically be refuted or mistaken, then knowledge is not present because knowledge requires 100 percent certainty. The skeptic believes avoiding error is better than gaining truth and believes he must be shown wrong before anyone can claim to know anything.

The *particularist* elevates the value of gaining as many truths as are available in the world and tries to rebut the skeptic. To rebut something is not to show that it is wrong but simply to show that the skeptic's argument has not adequately shown it to be true. The particularist places the burden of proof on the skeptic. He requires the skeptic to show his skepticism to be true and show it should be taken seriously before he allows the skeptic to bother him about knowledge. Given that the skeptic cannot consistently argue for his skepticism, there is no reason to deny what is obvious to all of us: that we do know many things.

ANSWERING SCIENTISM

We have all met people who don't believe something can be true unless it can be proven scientifically. Because most religious or ethical claims cannot be tested in the lab, these people assert that the claims cannot be known. This paradigm is known as scientism.

Scientism is the view that science is the only way to find truth and rationality. It holds that if information does not square with well-established scientific beliefs or cannot be verified with scientific methodology, then it is not true or rational. According to this view, everything outside of science is a matter of mere belief and subjective opinion, of which rational assessment is impossible. With the scientist, science is our exclusive model for intellectual excellence.

There are two forms of scientism: strong and weak. Strong scientism is the view that some proposition or theory is true or rational if and only if it is a scientific proposition or theory. Weak scientism allows for the existence of truths apart from science and is even willing to grant that they can have some minimal status for being rational without the support of science. But advocates of weak scientism still hold that science is the most valuable, serious, and authoritative sector of human learning and that every other intellectual activity is inferior to science. Further, in this view, there are virtually no limits to science. It can shed light on all fields of learning.

If either strong or weak scientism were true, we would not be able to integrate our scientific and theological beliefs. If strong scientism is true, then theology of any kind cannot be rational. If weak scientism is true, then we would have only a one-sided conversation in which theology would be listening to science and waiting for science to give it support. For Christians with smart faith, neither of these is acceptable.

WHERE SCIENTISM FAILS

We hope you'll get a kick out of this. Strong scientism destroys itself because it is self-refuting. Propositions that refer to and falsify themselves — for example, "There are no English sentences" and "There are no truths" — are self-refuting. (The first sentence *is* an English sentence, and the second sentence proposes a truth about truths.) Scientism is not a proposition of science; it is actually a proposition of philosophy about science and a proposition that only scientific propositions are true and/or rational. In other words, scientism is a philosophical claim and not a claim about science.

> You: I believe God is the creator of the world.
>
> Mr. Science: That cannot possibly be verified because God cannot be known through the use of science.
>
> You: So, you are claiming that unless science supports a claim, it cannot possibly be accepted as true?
>
> Mr. Science: Absolutely. Science is the only tool for determining truth. Philosophy and religion are useful only when supported by what science has made known.
>
> You: But isn't that a statement of philosophy to say truth can be determined only by science?
>
> Mr. Science: I suppose so. Does it matter?
>
> You: Well, if you say philosophy cannot be of use unless science

informs it, that statement is itself a philosophy that must be believed in order to hold that science can be your only source for determining truth.

Mr. Science: Hmmm . . .

This imaginary conversation shows that science cannot be practiced in thin air. Science itself relies on a number of foundations that must be assumed if science is ever to be useful. Each of the following assumptions of science has been challenged, but the task of stating and defending them is the job of philosophy, not science! This means the conclusions of science are no more truthful than the philosophies it uses to reach those conclusions. Here are some of those:

- The external world is orderly.
- The eternal world is knowable.
- Truth exists.
- Laws of logic exist.
- Human beings are reliable truth gatherers.
- Numbers and mathematical truths exist.

While we may never need to bring these up in conversation, we must mentally file the fact that science cannot do the work of science without consenting to certain philosophical assumptions.

Science also fails in that true and rationally justified beliefs exist in a host of fields outside of science. The laws of logic (something can't be true and false at the same time), moral absolutes (kindness is a virtue, not a vice), knowledge of my own consciousness (I'm feeling happy right now), knowledge from memory (I had eggs this morning), historical knowledge (Washington was the first U.S. president), and literary knowledge (Shakespeare was a gifted writer) are all examples of nonscientific knowledge. With this weakness of strong scientism in mind, we won't allow ourselves to be intimidated by the scientism argument. It just doesn't work.

We can take this two steps further. First, some propositions believed outside of science ("red is a color," "torturing babies is wrong," "I am now thinking about science") are better justified than some propositions believed within science ("evolution takes place through a series of very small steps"). Second, many of the beliefs now held in science will be revised or abandoned over the next hundred years, yet it is hard to imagine this happening to the just-mentioned beliefs outside of science.

ANSWERING MORAL RELATIVISM

Can two moral relativists define *moral relativism* in the same way and both be correct? Moral relativism implies that moral beliefs are not simply true or false but are relative to the beliefs of a given culture. For example, Society A may believe adultery is morally permissible and Society B may believe adultery is morally forbidden. So for those who are members of Society A, adultery is okay, and for Society B, it is morally forbidden. Described this way, moral relativism means that everyone should act according to their society's code (or perhaps to their own individual code).

Let's look at another example to clarify the definition further. Societies that believe murder is wrong could apply this belief in different ways: They may punish people based on different factors such as whether the murder was premeditated, an act of passion, and so on. But moral relativism goes beyond this diversity in a society. The point in understanding moral relativism is not that there is a certain relativity in the *application* of moral principles but that the moral propositions themselves are relative to a given culture.

When moral relativism is connected to a society's beliefs, we call it *conventionalism*; when it is dependent on individuals, it is called *subjectivism*. Conventionalism says moral truth is relative to entire cultures (for example, the state of Georgia does not recognize marriage between two individuals of the same sex). Subjectivism says moral truth is relative to the beliefs of each individual ("I'm gay and I should be able to get married").

FIVE OBJECTIONS TO MORAL RELATIVISM

Because of the seriousness of the criticisms raised against it, the majority of moral philosophers and theologians do not embrace moral relativism. What is amazing, however, is how many people in the world live like moral relativists. We will encounter many people who are moral relativists—whether they realize it or not—so we need to pay careful attention to these objections.

1. It is difficult to define what a society is or what the relevant society is. Consider our first example regarding adultery in Society A and Society B. Assume that a married woman from Society A (where adultery is permissible) meets a man from Society B (where adultery is forbidden). How do you determine whose beliefs are wrong?

2. Another problem, similar to the first, is that we are often simultaneously members of several different societies that may hold different moral values: our nuclear family, extended family, neighborhood, school, church, work, county, state, country, and so on. Which of these society's values are we supposed to follow? Many of us have been in different church cultures; for example, there are churches where alcohol consumption by any member is forbidden, and there are churches where drinking in moderation even takes place on the church property! What do we do in this case?

3. Moral relativism suffers from a problem known as "the reformer's dilemma." Moral reformers are those who look at a society's code and pronounce a need for reform and change in that code, often providing arguments to support their view. If moral relativism were true, it's logically impossible for a society to have a virtuous moral reformer such as Jesus, Gandhi, or Martin Luther King Jr. If an act is right only if it is in keeping with a given society's code, then the moral reformer by definition is an immoral person, for his views are at odds with society. Any view that implies the existence of a moral reformer is impossible must be defective because we know that these reformers have existed. In other words, moral relativism implies that neither cultures nor individuals can improve their moral code; the only thing they can do is change it.

4. Some acts are wrong regardless of social conventions. When we argue this point, we are basically holding to the particularist view (see our earlier discussion on skepticism, pages 120-123) to claim that all people can know that some things are wrong—witnessing a crime but doing nothing about it, stealing food from starving orphans, using a pet for target practice—without first needing criteria for knowing how it is we know such things. In this case, an act can be wrong and known to be wrong even when a society says it is right. And an act can be right and known to be right even when a society says it is wrong. In fact, an act can be right or wrong even when a society says nothing about it.

5. If moral relativism were true, one society can't easily be justified in morally blaming another society. In this scenario, we should obey our society's moral codes and others should obey their society's moral codes. So, if Mr. Smith does what's right in his code but wrong in mine, how can we criticize his

act as wrong? From Hitler to Saddam Hussein, we as nations would have no justification to criticize the treatment of people within those cultures or impose human rights violations on any other country.

For these reasons, moral relativism must be rejected. It's up to you to understand why moral relativism doesn't work and to challenge others who claim it. Here's a real-life example of how a challenge could look:

J. P.: According to the Bible, all of us are guilty of sin and we will be punished unless we place our faith in the death of Christ to pay for our sins.

Student: Hey, man, whatever works for you is true for you, and whatever works for me is true for me. If something works for you, great, but you shouldn't force your moral views on other people.

J. P.: Wow. You really believe that? Well, then, thanks for your time. I'll go now. [As J. P. walks out the door, he grabs the student's stereo and takes it with him.]

Student: Hey! That's my stereo. You can't take that.

J. P.: I know I'm a little older than you, but I do jog regularly and lift weights, so I most certainly "can" take this. What I think you mean is that I "should not" take your stereo.

Student: Yeah—you shouldn't take it! That's stealing.

J. P.: Well, I need a stereo for my Bible study. Yours looks good to me. Taking it may be wrong for you, but I have no trouble taking your stereo with me. Now, seeing that it's wrong to force our beliefs on others, don't you think you would be wrong to force your belief on me that stealing is wrong?

Student: Uhhh, hang on.

J. P.: You know what I think? I think you claim that morality is relative only in areas where it is convenient for you, such as sexual morality, or in other areas you don't care about, like religion. But when it comes to someone stealing your stereo, I'll bet you become a moral absolutist pretty quickly, don't you?

Student: I suppose you have a point there.

A true story: This student eventually saw the inconsistency of his behavior, and a few weeks later, I (J. P.) was able to lead him to Jesus Christ.

MENTAL GYMNASTICS

The kind of thinking this chapter requires—about the beliefs of skepticism, scientism, and moral relativism—is practical and beneficial because we face opposition like this almost every time we discuss our faith in Christ. Contending with these issues requires some exercise in the mental gym, and we must commit to the regimen. Our efforts will build some serious muscle for rationally defending Christianity.

Remember, though, that we shouldn't work out alone. Exercising our minds in community with other believers is a requirement. We need others as partners to challenge our arguments and thinking and to show us fresh strategies.

SMART THINKING

As we have mentioned in previous chapters, 1 Peter 3:15 commands us to be ready to give a reasoned defense to someone who asks us for a credible reason why we believe what we do. Can you do it? Right now? Explain in three simple, intelligent sentences what you believe? Without using Scripture? Without talking about feelings?

If you find your heart racing and your mind stuttering, then take the time to brainstorm your reasons on a sheet of paper. After you've done that, look at your list and highlight the three reasons you think most convincing. Practice those reasons and be ready to give them at any opportunity. And make sure that you can elaborate on your concise reasons should anyone ask you for more information!

To follow is an example. We recommend you brainstorm your own reasons first, to avoid getting stuck on these reasons. Also, just because you have three good reasons doesn't mean they won't be challenged, so be ready! After all, if someone actually asks you for your reasons, God is going to use you to make an impact.

1. I believe because the evidence—historical, archaeological, scientific, and so on—for Christianity is more credible than the evidence for other faiths (or no faith at all).
2. I believe because Christianity is the only philosophy that explains every aspect of the realities in our world: human beings and nature, evil and good, love and hate, liberty and bondage, creativity and ingenuity, and so on.
3. I believe because I have asked for God's involvement in my life and, as a result, have experienced His responses, too many responses to be labeled coincidence.

CHAPTER EIGHT

DOES QUIET TIME MEAN "ZZZZZ" TO US?

WAKING UP OUR PERSONAL STUDY AND DEVOTION

Very early in the morning, while it was still dark, Jesus got up, left the house and went off to a solitary place, where he prayed.

MARK 1:35

Shock rippled over the faces of the campers surrounding me (Mark). What had I said for them to look at me this way? We had reached the last day of a weeklong summer camp where I was the speaker. One of the church groups had invited me to come to their cabin after the morning session to answer some questions. The first question was, "What do you do for a quiet time?"

I asked them exactly what they meant by quiet time, and they defined it as a time in the morning when a person reads the Bible and prays. I told them I didn't have a quiet time, and they looked, well, disappointed. Before they could burn me at the stake for claiming to be a minister of the gospel and not having a quiet time, I asked them a question (a trick I learned from Jesus). "How many of you have a quiet time every morning?" The room was silent (an absence of sound frequently experienced by Jesus in response to His questions).

I asked another question, "Why don't you have a quiet time?" The campers offered several answers to this one: that quiet times didn't seem to accomplish anything in their lives, that waking up in the morning was too difficult, and so on. I then asked, "Why do you think a quiet time is important?" The students responded, "Because you need to read the Bible. Prayer is really important. You need to spend time with God every day." So they believed quiet times were important, but they just couldn't get them going.

These students had a desire to know God and understood that spending time with Him was critical to doing that, but something wasn't working. In this chapter, we're going to explore how to develop a daily spiritual walk, but hopefully it will look different from what you've always thought of as a quiet time.

THE TYPICAL QUIET TIME

Just like these students, most people think that time spent with God each day needs to be early in the morning. And why not? For centuries, Christians have started their day with a time of biblical reflection. The Bible tells us that Jesus often arose early to be alone and to pray. Spending time with God early in the morning makes sense given that throughout history, most of the world has lived in an agricultural society. Without access to electrical power, most people went to bed early and woke up early. We live in a world today where people stay up much later because we have the ability to light our way into the night. Many people even work all night long.

Most Americans also enjoy the comfort of personal space — something that few in the world have experienced up until the last century. The ability to have a quiet moment away from others was difficult unless it occurred early in the day.

The sad thing about this discussion is that it reveals we have compartmentalized our time with God to a small portion of the day. While devoted time is necessary and rewarding, we should be in communion with God throughout our day. You may be mentally alert in the evening. That's great. Spend concentrated time with God then. For others, the morning may indeed work best. That's fine, too. But whenever you do have time with God, be sure to spend devoted time with Him and refuse to allow your fellowship with Him to exist only within that small time frame in your life.

BIBLE READING

For most of history, individuals didn't have personal access to Scripture. Scripture was kept in certain places, such as the synagogue or the temple, and people went there to hear Scriptures read aloud. It wasn't until the 1450s, with the invention of the printing press by Johann Gutenberg, that Bibles and written teaching were available to the masses for personal study.

The freeing of individual minds to read and think about Scripture paved the way for Christianity to mature and grow. It is a real privilege to be able to read Scripture in our own homes. We need to take advantage of this tremendous blessing, but we must find a productive way to do it.

PRAYER

To be able to communicate directly with God is an incredible opportunity that most of us underutilize. The classic prayers of David in the book of Psalms are great examples of real-life situations being presented to God. Just like David, in prayer we experience intimacy with God. We come to Him in joy, thankfulness, confusion, anger, exhaustion, and so on. Then if we listen, He responds to us and we come away fresh. Prayer exposes us for who we are in light of God's majesty, and it aligns our lives with who God is.

If this description of prayer isn't quite what you've experienced, let's find out what's missing.

THE NOT-SO-TYPICAL QUIET TIME

Up to this point, I've presented a simplistic overview of what makes a typical quiet time. While the components seem solid, what is missing in our lives that could enhance our experience, promote our intellectual development, and draw us nearer to our Creator? So often we impose a system or formulaic structure to our time with God rather than giving it the space to be a living, breathing experience of truth with the living God as He transforms our lives.

What we have come to call quiet time is simply individual worship of God. While setting a regular time to do these worship activities is important (in part because it creates a habit), God desires that our whole life be filled with habits to develop a love for Him—habits that involve our heart, mind, and soul. Here are some helpful disciplines we're suggesting you incorporate into your life *and* your time alone with God.

Solitude

Quiet is the one thing missing in most quiet times. Solitude keeps our quiet time from becoming another task to be scheduled into our hurried lives and checked off our to-do lists. A walk alone can make for a great time of solitude. (We talked earlier about how it can help stimulate you at low-energy points of your day.) But you don't have to walk. Sitting still in a room, as strange as it may sound to us in this busy world, is perfectly acceptable. Watching television, even with the sound off, doesn't qualify.

STUDY

In any human endeavor, repetitive exercise and practice bring skill and excellence. Specific activities can be beneficial because they accomplish specific results: For example, swinging a baseball bat is good if it produces a base hit. That same activity can also be done for general training: A person can repeatedly swing a bat in a batting cage to improve his game. That same activity can also provide other good results, even unintended: Regular trips to the batting cage can improve a person's physical condition.

The same thing is true for study, which can and should be a part of your normal life. We often correctly approach study for some specific end — say, a test we have to take or a paper we have to prepare. But if we read and study only things we must, such as homework assignments, we lose a great opportunity to develop the mind-enriching skills relevant to growing as a person in general.

Choose to study subjects in Scripture other than those that are immediately interesting to you or meet a need. Pick an obscure book of the Bible and really wrestle with what God is trying to reveal to you. Read through the book you choose from beginning to end. When you do Bible study, don't skip passages and verses that don't make sense or don't seem related to your life. Make some notes on those, pray about them, and seek other input to help you understand. (Buying a companion guide, if available, may also help you.) Ask your pastor or youth pastor to help you find some helpful Bible study tools to understand Scripture better.

PRAYER

Anytime we articulate our thoughts, feelings, and desires, the mind is engaged. This happens so wonderfully in the act of prayer. Have you ever felt like you knew exactly what you thought about something but then when you sat down to write it or share it with another, you realized that you hadn't completely thought through the matter? I (Mark) have had this experience many times—when writing papers in college and when writing books. There is a sense in me that I have great command of what I want to say until it comes down to actually saying it!

Prayer is the act of reflecting on our lives and communicating our experience to God. One of the greatest things you can do is write your prayers out. You'll find you don't drift off, and you will keep from repeating the same ideas over and over again. As a bonus, you can write down what you hear God saying to you. Looking back over what you write can help you evaluate whether what you wrote was really "God's voice" as well as let you see answers to your prayers and how your faith matures over time. It can give you an objective view of your thoughts that would be otherwise impossible.

Planetwisdom.com hosts a week of online prayer every spring. Students log on to prayer chat rooms and type in their prayers. Students have commented how easy it is to pray when they are doing so in a chat room. Writing your words better engages your mind in the prayer process.

OBSERVATION

Solomon acquired great understanding by making accurate observations about life and nature. In the first chapter of Ecclesiastes, he observed patterns of nature, such as the rising of the sun and the evaporation of the oceans. In doing so, he recognized the temporary nature of man as contrasting with the seeming permanence of nature: "Generations come and generations go, but the earth remains forever" (verse 4). This observation led him to a further insight: Because our lives on this earth are so short, our only hope for meaning and significance is if we live for what's permanent: God and His kingdom.

In the tradition of Solomon, we too should learn to observe

nature, people, and God and seek new truths in such observations. When you go about your day, are you rushing to your next task and the next person you need to meet, or are you taking time to enjoy and evaluate the scenery of life? Developing the mind is not simply about reaching a destination; it is about a thoughtful, God-directed journey that will make our time here worthwhile.

TAKING THOUGHTS CAPTIVE

We must realize that we are strangers in a foreign land and then live according to that reality. Captive Daniel and his friends from Israel provide a good example for us. Ideas will always exist in our culture and this world that will be in strong opposition to those of God revealed both in nature and through Scripture. Because Daniel's mind and faith were mature, God was able to use him as a powerful representative amid the foreign Babylonian culture.

In the same way, we need not shy away from the culture we find ourselves in but rather be ready to engage it. When it comes to movies, television, music, and literature, are we prepared to take an active role (versus watching, listening, or reading passively) to demolish arguments that go against the Lord? Are we ready to take thoughts captive to the obedience of Christ, as we are instructed to do in 2 Corinthians 10:5? As we learned in chapter 7, demolishing an argument requires more than protesting against things we know are wrong. We must use our minds and reason (such as the principles of logic) to find the weakness of the argument in question.

To do this, we must ask several questions. First, what, if anything, does this piece of art tell me about the character of God? If the work in question does make claims about the nature or character of God, what is consistent or inconsistent with God's revelation of Himself in nature and Scripture? Second, what does this work tell me about life? Art of every kind makes moral claims. Are these morals consistent with Scripture? Why or why not? Art also makes claims about what is significant in life. Are these consistent with Scripture? Why or why not? Finally, art represents ideas about how life works. Are these ideas consistent with what we see in reality and from Scripture?

By evaluating the ideas we put into our minds (and talking them over with God), we move out of the passive role of merely viewing and absorbing information into an active role—analyzing the information—that engages the intellect. When using our minds becomes a normal part of our lives, we will gain continual insight as to how we can best respond as Christians to the world in which we live.

MEANINGFUL TIME WITH GOD

The reason many students struggle with daily quiet times is that the quiet times are rarely interesting or challenging enough to be worthwhile. In fact, church culture has made the Christian life out to be so easy and carefree that it has become only a shadow of itself.

In reality, the Christian life is deep and mysterious and meaningful. So we need to forget the lukewarm Christianity we may have been sold and instead use these activities to transform a mundane quiet time into a daily practice robust with meaning as well as intellectual and spiritual growth. Stepping up to the challenge in our daily times with God is a habit that will lead to spiritual maturity.

SMART THINKING

Take a moment and reflect on and answer these questions:

1. How can time alone with God be your personal worship of Him?

2. When was the last time you spent time alone with God? Describe that time (frustrating, rewarding, satisfying).
3. How often, if at all, do you have time alone with God? How often would you like to spend time with Him?
4. Do you really want to have quiet time? If not, why? If yes, when will you do it and how will you spend that time?

If you do not have regular time alone with God, take at least ten minutes today to practice. Think about how you might incorporate this activity into your daily life. If you already have a quiet time, begin incorporating the ideas we discussed in this chapter into the time you have.

Whether you are new to spending time alone with God or are someone who needs to renew your time alone with God, remember not to worry or give up if nothing seems to happen those first few times you sit in silence before Him. Consider the possibility that God is testing your resolve. Resist being someone who needs instant gratification, and hang in there until your experience comes to life.

CHAPTER NINE

CLOSE COMMUNICATION

REFOCUSING OUR WORSHIP

Take my intellect, and use Every Power as thou shalt choose.
FROM THE HYMN "TAKE MY LIFE AND LET IT BE"

Worship is about God and building Him up. But we often focus on what we can get out of worship instead of what we can offer to Him. Maturing in our faith and deepening our relationship with our Lord means, in part, that we wrestle our inward focus outward and up. A developed mind will help us worship in a way God desires.

But what is worship? We are most familiar with the worship that includes specific acts of praise, typically expressed through singing and public readings and usually in assembly with other people of God. This is indeed worship, but it is only one aspect of it. True worship is much more than this.

Worship means to intentionally credit God with worth, service, and reverence. Worship can take place individually (such as in our time alone with God) and corporately (such as in church worship and fellowship with other believers). For believers whose faith is fully integrated into their lives, however, everything about them is an act of worship. When our faith is integrated, worship is expressed in our overall approach to life and in every aspect of that life (see Romans 12:1). Worship creates a home for our souls as we learn to rest in God. As Isaiah 26:3 promises, "You will keep in perfect peace him whose mind is steadfast, because he trusts in you."

This holistic worship is the one we need to seek. When we give proper credit to God, when we give our whole selves, we reap the positive by-products, such as healthy, well-developed minds. In fact, we can't worship fully without continuing to develop our minds.

WORSHIPING THE MAXIMALLY PERFECT BEING

Think about a student who reveres a basketball player. Because the athlete is good at what he does, he is worthy of this student's respect and adoration. If the basketball player is incompetent and performs poorly, the student might like the player, but it would be inappropriate for the student to revere him. What we mean is that a person should proportion out respect based on the worthiness of the object of the respect. Let's say another basketball player came along with superior skill to the first we mentioned. The student would owe more reverence to this player than he would to the other player.

This simple insight about respect actually holds great implications for our worship of God. Theologians describe God as a maximally perfect being. This means that God is not merely the greatest, most perfect being who happens to exist but He is the greatest being who *could possibly* exist! If God were merely the greatest being who happened to exist, it would be possible for a greater god to come along (even if such a being did not actually exist) or for the real God to grow in His excellence. If God were merely the greatest being who happened to exist, then He would not be a worthy object of total worship.

The God of the Bible, however, is *the* maximally perfect being. It is impossible for anyone to take His place as greater, a truth that makes idol worship a serious sin. When we worship an idol, we give more dedication to something finite and inferior than we do to God. As the maximally perfect being, God alone is worthy of the best efforts we can give in worshiping Him. We must offer our total selves, including our minds.

When we consider what we "owe" God in worship, we discover that dedication to intellectual growth is not primarily for our benefit; instead, it is an act of service to God. Developing our minds is part of worship. When we slack off mentally in any area—high school, college, Bible study, work, youth group—then our worship of God starves. So, how can we bring our minds into worship?

CORPORATE WORSHIP

How many times have we stood in the congregation singing but not really connecting with the words of the song? What makes us leave our minds at home when we come together to worship God? Perhaps it's partly habit—no one (including ourselves) requires us to involve our minds—and perhaps it's partly encouragement just "to feel," to have an experience. Well, this halfhearted worship is unacceptable to God—there's no other way to put it. But we're not left in the dark. Scripture tells us what is acceptable.

WORSHIP IN SPIRIT AND TRUTH

In John 4, Jesus met a woman by a well who was from a different race than the Jews. She was a Samaritan. Jesus' encounter with this woman is rich with meaning, but we will focus on the woman's misunderstanding regarding the nature of worship. The woman stated in verse 20, "Our fathers worshiped on this mountain, but you Jews claim that the place where we must worship is in Jerusalem."

Jesus responded, "God is spirit, and those who worship Him must worship in spirit and truth" (verse 24, NASB). By this, Jesus meant that worship that really counts is not based on how we conform to the customs of community. Instead, worship occurs in our inner beings. Worship must be sincere, earnest, and consistent with the true nature of God, His revelation, and His acts.

The first part of the verse, "God is spirit," forms the foundation on which Jesus' entire response is built. In Greek, when an author wanted to emphasize an adjective (in this case, *spirit*), he would place it at the beginning of the sentence. So the phrase could be restated this way: "It is of first importance to recognize that God's very nature is that of spiritual being." But why is this phrase so relevant to the nature of genuine worship? In John's writings, we often come across words and phrases that have dual meanings, both that are intended by the author. For example, in John 3:7, Jesus says we must be "born *anothen*." The Greek term *anothen* can mean either "again" or "from above," and the double meaning appears to be intentional.

There is a double meaning, too, in "God is *pneuma* [spirit]." Jesus meant two things by *spirit*. First, God is a spiritual being (not made of matter). Because material objects such as idols are located at specific places, it makes sense to localize worship to where idols are. But because God is an omnipresent spirit, He is not limited to time and space, making a specific location unnecessary for worship.

The second meaning of *spirit* in the passage is more relevant to our topic. Throughout the Old Testament, God is often referred to as spirit to emphasize that He is a living, active being who initiates involvement with His creations and gives them life. Thus, in Genesis 1:2, it is the spirit of God who hovers over the waters. In John's writing, this same meaning is frequently associated with God the Spirit. In John 6:63, it is the Spirit who gives life, and in John 7:37-39, it is the Spirit who produces rivers of living water in the lives of God's children. We learn through this analysis that worship is not under our control, nor is the form worship takes. Rather, worship is a response to God who initiates toward us, gives us life, and shows Himself active on our behalf.

For example, if God initiates worship, and our response to God is our worship, then it would make sense for the worship portion of a church service to take place later in the service — after we have heard the Scripture message and after we have heard testimony of what God has done in people's lives during the week. But because most churches schedule worship near the beginning of the service, and because we may have no control over that, we need to prepare our hearts beforehand to make sure our part of the worship is truly a response to God. One way we can do that is by having our own "pre-service" prior to attending church. We can include some time spent reading His Word (such as last week's lesson or, if the pastor is doing a series, the next Scripture), sharing with family and friends about what God is doing in our life, or listening to worship music.

WORSHIP WITH MUSIC

Another way to enhance our intellectual engagement in worship has to do with the music itself: the lyrics and the type of songs. We don't have just one kind of song to sing to God. The Bible shows different lyrics and different purposes for singing. In our private worship we need to find an appropriate balance, and in corporate worship we must be in agreement to the words, not just participate in the singing.

The content of songs is important. Some songs are for intensifying believers' unity. Other songs share our thirst for knowing more of God. Many songs allow us to convey deep emotions to God. Still others convey doctrinal truths affirming what we believe.

The type of song can be important, too. Simple praise songs might focus on repeating basic truths, while hymns and other songs often include complex lyrics and deeper theological truths.

Being discerning about songs helps us become intentional about what we do in another aspect of our faith. Again, we can't control the order, type, and content of songs for worship during a church service, but we're free to do that with our own Christian CDs. If we're going to worship God privately with music rather than merely stringing some favorite songs together, we should choose specific songs, in a specific order, for a specific purpose in our worship. The songs we choose, for example, could focus on God's power, Christ's sacrifice, or the Holy Spirit's inspiration. The variations are endless.

WORSHIP IN CLOSE RELATIONSHIP

In Ephesians 5:31-32, Paul compares the sexual one-flesh relationship in marriage between a man and a woman to Christ's relationship with the church. In an interesting way, the people of God are married to Christ, and because of that, idolatry is called adultery throughout the Bible. If this seems like a strange comparison, hang on. In an ideal marriage relationship, there is devotion and fidelity, a commitment of one party to the other with no cheating taking place. And fidelity, openness, mutual adoration, and tenderness are the basis of a great sexual relationship.

But if a husband and wife jump into bed together, quickly have intercourse, and then go their separate ways, the fulfillment God intended for that union would certainly be absent. When two people are simply seeking to get their needs met, sex quickly becomes a chore rather than a celebration of love. Early in my (Mark's) marriage, I traveled a lot without my wife, occasionally for long periods. Starting where we left off when I got home was not easy. We had to spend some time talking and sharing. For example, sometimes we would take a walk and hold hands. We would rekindle the fire of our relationship before jumping ahead to the most intimate aspect of our relationship.

Unfortunately, our relationship with God can be just like the one between distant spouses. Often we simply attend church, do the tasks we're supposed to do, and then go back to all our separate activities of the week. What kind of relationship with God is that? Maybe that's why worship during conferences and camps can be so much richer than what we experience on Sunday. An environment solely devoted to focusing on God (corporately and individually) for an extended period of time allows us to reacquaint ourselves with our Maker — to remember who He is and what He has done for us. Through fellowship with other believers and this special focused time, we are drawn toward deep intimacy with our Creator.

But we can't wait for camp or conferences to develop a healthy, intimate relationship with Him. We must regularly work on our relationship so that we grow ever closer.

WORSHIP IN SUPPLICATION

We need to use our minds more carefully in supplication before God. *Supplication* is the practice of reasoning with Him. The fact that the Lord allows us to reason with Him is remarkable. Our God actually desires for us to know Him and His ways! We don't have to guess at what He might prefer or how He might act.

I (Mark) remember my dad asking me to feed my brother's rabbits. Because this was not my job, I asked him why. Now, there may have been many reasonable responses he could have given, but he said, "Because I said so." No doubt you have heard similar words from your parents. While our earthly fathers and mothers have the authority to make us do things that are unreasonable, God never demands that we do something just because He says so (even though He has every right!). Everything God requires of us is within reason. And He gives us the privilege of reasoning with Him.

Martin Luther said that "in 'supplication' we strengthen prayer and make it effective by a certain form of persuasion."[21] Scripture regularly portrays supplication as a way of approaching God in which we bring our "case" before God (see Jeremiah 12:1; 20:12). The Hebrew word for *case* is *rib*, and it means a reasoned legal case brought before a judge. In supplication, we need to carefully think through our requests and the reasons behind them before we approach God. We then reason our case before His throne and trust He will consider our request.

Focused and coherent reasoning is important to supplication. We want to avoid vague and rambling prayers. Have you ever heard a prayer that referred to God as Father and then later thanked Him for dying on the cross? God the Father did not die on the cross! This kind of mistake is actually a heresy known as patripassianism. Prayers like that reveal the wandering mind of the prayer leader. Of course, we may address the entire Godhead of the triune God in prayer, but we should be clear in our minds whom we are addressing. If we decide to specify one person of the Trinity, we need to be clear about that, too.

C. S. Lewis captured the issue of unfocused prayer in *The Screwtape Letters* when the demon Screwtape wrote his demon nephew Wormwood about Wormwood's Christian "patient." Wormwood is instructed to have his "patient"

> remember, or to think he remembers, the parrot-like nature of his prayers in childhood. In reaction against that, he may be persuaded to aim at something entirely spontaneous, inward, informal, and unregulated, and what this will actually mean to a beginner will be an effort to produce in himself a vaguely devotional mood in which real concentration of will and intelligence have no part.[22]

Some of us may believe that the Spirit is more authentically experienced when we are spontaneous and unprepared in our prayers. But because supplication is a form of reasoned persuasion before God, this can't be true. We must be deliberate in challenging our minds to form better prayers, especially when we gather with other believers. Doing so means we might need to write out a carefully prepared prayer to read during the prayer time.

WORSHIP IN FELLOWSHIP

When you think of Aristotle, the philosopher and follower of Plato, friendship probably isn't the first thing to pop into your mind. But according to Aristotle, there are three kinds of friendship: those based on usefulness and advantage, those based on pleasure, and those based on goodness.[23] The first two do not necessarily involve people who genuinely feel affection for each other. The only goal in those relationships is to gain something from them. The third type of friendship Aristotle observed is starkly different. These friendships are formed around common visions, common virtues, and the pursuit of the good life. In this type of friendship, the goal is to strengthen and sustain each other in commitment and progress to a life well lived.

In his observations on this type of friendship, Aristotle had discovered God's truth about the importance of connecting with other people holding common values. Without the Word of God, however, friendship lacks the environment needed to foster the good life: fellowship in the body of Christ. The New Testament's concept of friendship deepens and fulfills the truth Aristotle observed.

The word *fellowship* is used to translate the Greek word *koinonia*, which has a root meaning "to hold something in common." In Jesus' time, this word primarily referred to those who joined together through financial participation in support of the spread of the gospel (see Philippians 1:5). Today we expand the word to mean "joining together for developing commitment to and advancing the kingdom of God and the gospel of Christ."

This understanding of fellowship sheds light on the time we

spend with other believers. Fellowship does not mean people getting together simply to enjoy one another and have a good time, although there is nothing wrong with that in the right context. In true fellowship, our minds are engaged as we meet together to discuss how to grow in our understanding of Christ's teaching, defend our beliefs, break out of godless patterns of thinking, spread the good news to unbelievers, and so on.

Fellowship can be powerful when we leverage it to accomplish its purposes, but diminishing its power is dangerously easy. We must guard against turning it into purely entertainment as well as allowing an inward focus that neglects the advancement of the gospel.

Excellence in Worship

If you have ever visited Disneyland or Disney World, you know that the experience is impressive. Literally, every aspect of these theme parks is intentionally orchestrated—from the decoration, to the uniforms worn by the employees, to the food that is served, to the music played throughout the park. The goal is to create an excellent environment. Meeting this goal even includes the way lightbulbs are handled! In order to keep anyone visiting the park from seeing a burned out lightbulb, Disney has employed an entire crew of "lampers" to change each bulb when it is only about 80 percent expired. That is excellence!

How can we offer less excellence than Disney when it comes to worshiping the living God? We need to give Him everything we've got.

SMART THINKING

First, think about a request you'd like to make before God. Maybe there is a friend you'd like to see know Christ. Maybe there is something that you really need. Reread the section from this chapter on supplication and write out your case before God. Use Scripture, what you know of God's character, and what God has done for you in the past to reason your case before Him.

Second, think about your believing friends. Would you describe your interaction as *koinonia*? Write down ways you can make your fellowship more meaningful as well as how you can leverage it for its intended purposes.

WHERE DO WE
SHUT OUT GOD?

APPLYING OUR MINDS TO HOME,
SCHOOL, WORK, AND PLAY

*We are therefore Christ's ambassadors, as though God were
making his appeal through us.*

2 CORINTHIANS 5:20

I (Mark) fly a lot—so much so that I have been granted Elite
Flyer status on several airlines. I know the system; I know airports.
One morning I did my typical trip to Dallas–Fort Worth. I know
exactly how long it will take me to get to the airport and my gate from
my front door, and this knowledge even allows for inconveniences
such as traffic jams or the newbie traveler. He's the one wearing a suit
of armor and having troubles getting through the security checkpoint,
completely baffled that all the metal on his body is problematic.

But on this particular Friday, the airline had launched a new
e-mail ticket program, and the staff was adjusting to the sudden
change. I arrived at the airport to find long lines and rampant confusion everywhere I turned. Needless to say, I was not a happy Elite

Flyer! Instead of being hurried through a line for Elite Flyers and offered a complimentary upgrade, I was told to be patient and wait in an extremely long line. I watched as irate customer after irate customer approached the counter only to be met by a hopelessly confused employee tapping on the computer, dumbfounded that the machine was unresponsive. I was convinced I could make more progress on the computer with a blindfold and rubber mallet than this woman. What is more, I am a frequent flyer, one of the elite — this was no way to treat your best customers!

I prepared a vicious speech to deliver when I approached the counter. I got ready to let this lady have a piece of my mind (or what little was left of it at the moment). But as I waited for the unsatisfied customer in front of me to be assisted, God interrupted my mental preparation by tapping on my heart. He said, "Mark, you do not represent 'Mark Matlock, Frequent Flyer.' You represent Me. Remember that." Immediately, I knew He was right. The words of my nasty speech faded away. I had been thinking of my status instead of being the example of Christ described in Philippians 2:6: "Who being in very nature God, did not consider equality with God something to be grasped." If Christ was able to set aside his power position to be a servant, I would need to as well. Just in time; I was up next.

I approached the counter with a smile and asked the airline employee how her day was going. She responded that it was going badly and she was frustrated she couldn't do a better job of helping her customers. I told her I was fine with her service and offered to pray for her as I boarded the plane. The frantic look passed from her face, and she thanked me. I did not have time (nor would it have been appropriate) to share the gospel at that moment, but at least I was able to give her a quick glimpse of Christ.

As I walked toward the plane, I prayed for her, but I also apologized to the Lord for having placed my travel experience into a separate compartment from my faith. We miss opportunities daily to advance the kingdom of God and live righteously because we keep Him in one sector of our life and go about our business without Him in the other sectors. If we are seeking what is described as an integrated life, this way of living is not it!

One of the great issues facing our generation is the separation of the spiritual and secular aspects of life. Devotion to God is usually limited to personal time spent with Him and time we set aside (like church, youth group, and so on) to focus on Him. More and more of us are forgetting that being a true disciple of Christ means that Christ and His teachings impact every part of our lives. Whether at church, home, school, work, or play, we are called to live the Christian life with excellence.

Integrating smart faith into our everyday living requires considerable thought and intention. Without this quality in our life, our faith stagnates because its power to transform our entire life has been stifled.

OPPORTUNITIES TO ALLOW GOD INTO OUR LIVES

A circumstance that seems like a challenge is often actually an opportunity. Consider these situations and how you might solve each person's dilemma.

Brandon loves soccer. He has a real talent for this and has built great relationships with others through his passion for the sport. Unfortunately, few Christians participate on his team. Plus, his youth pastor looks down on him because, due to his commitment to his team, he rarely has time to attend youth group functions. Is Brandon less spiritual because of his decision to pursue a sport with excellence?

Makenzie has a dream to one day go into acting for commercials and film. She hopes to move to California and somehow become involved in the industry. Even though she is a talented actress, members of her church have told her that Hollywood dreams are difficult to achieve without significant moral compromise. Should she pursue these dreams?

Clayton is a solid young man who enjoys playing video games. He likes online games best because he can play with other people rather than just by himself. On the weekends, his friends get together in his basement, hook up their Xboxes to one another, and play Halo all night long. A member of the church has spoken out against his playing. Is it possible that Clayton's activities could be important to advancing the kingdom?

Jane's parents are not followers of Christ. While they really do nothing to prevent her from attending church or pursuing her faith, she has problems with them at home because they tend to be much more strict than the parents of her friends. They often criticize her because of her beliefs, and this causes friction that usually leads to emotional explosions. What should her attitude be toward her folks?

J. T. attends a Christian school, which means he is constantly required to learn about the Bible through classes and chapels. He and his friends have "heard it all before" when it comes to living for Christ and are more inclined, frankly, to do the opposite of what they know is right when they're not at school. Most of them have learned to put on the mask and the happy face to appease their parents and teachers, but really they don't think much about Christianity outside of school. After all, they hear it all the time. J. T. knows there must be something else about his faith that he is not experiencing, but what is it?

Chad has a laptop that his school assigned him. Last week he discovered that he could use it to connect to his neighbor's wireless network and view pornography over the Internet in the seclusion of his bedroom. Nobody has any idea of what he is doing, and he has decided that he really isn't hurting anyone anyway.

Lauren walks past her neighbor's house every day. She knows that the lady living there is alone and recently had surgery. But it isn't her problem, so she just minds her own business and walks on by every day.

Josh just got an internship working for an ophthalmologist in town. He's excited because he hopes to pursue some type of medical field in the future. During his afternoon visits with the doctor, he realizes that most people in the medical community seem unconcerned about spiritual matters, such as how their faith impacts their practice.

Nicole has a teacher at school who is hostile toward Christianity. Everything the teacher presents in class completely disregards or even denigrates God and definitely does not take His Word or existence into account. Nicole has challenged the teacher on the matter by raising her hand and responding to certain issues with a Christian viewpoint, but the teacher has only made her feel ignorant. Nicole has decided that maybe God is better kept at church and not in academic life.

These students face unique problems integrating their faith into their life. Holistic living and spiritual growth are at stake. Their opportunity from God is in their crisis: If they choose easy ways out (the paths of least resistance), they will slow their progress, but if they recognize the right path, they'll speed toward that place where God is in every aspect of their life.

We are like these students. If our turn with such a dilemma hasn't come, it will. Recognizing the tempting wrong paths and the right path now will help us as we face the challenges.

PART II: Applying Our Smarts

HOW WE INTEGRATE — OR NOT

THE SECLUDED CHRISTIAN

This person is afraid of being influenced by the world and avoids it at all costs. He has no non-Christian friends, and he reads only Christian books and listens to only Christian music.

We must love the world as Christ did. Jesus did not avoid the world at all. In fact, Jesus associated with sinners so much that the religious leaders condemned Him for it (see Matthew 11:19). But Jesus showed love, not judgment, to sinners. He warned that judgment would come but that His purpose for those who followed Him was to save them from that judgment (see John 3:16-17).

While life may seem safe for the Secluded Christian, he will miss opportunities to be used by God. It is God's desire that we reflect His truth and love to a hurting world. Matthew 5:13-16 says we are called to be the salt of the earth and the light of the world. God has placed us in the world to be salt and light, give it flavor, and show the way. We can do this only if we are involved and not secluded.

J. T. is experiencing a lack of satisfaction in his life because he is secluded and not interacting in a healthy way as a Christian in the world. Even ministers can get so wrapped up in interacting only with Christians that they lose touch with the world until they no longer understand or relate to those who are lost.

Jane is a student who is having a hard time connecting with her parents because she is living two lives — one in the church and with church friends, and one outside church. This means she is losing the connection with her parents. Lauren, too, is so into her church life that she has little connection with her own neighbor.

Others — specifically Brandon, Makenzie, and Clayton — are not secluded, but they run the very real risk of going in another direction: becoming worldly.

THE WORLDLY CHRISTIAN

This person tries to balance being like the world and being a Christian. He desires to be like Christ but refuses to give up the things of this world. He is trying to save his life on earth but will ultimately lose it (see Matthew 16:25-26; Colossians 2:8).

The concept of being worldly has little to do with what we look like or who we spend time with and more to do with how we think. Some wrongly accuse those who attend movies, wear the latest fashions, and hang out with non-Christians as being worldly. But living according to the world means that we live according to a pattern that is neither correct nor healthy. It is this worldly pattern that Romans 12:2 refers to and advocates a transformed mind to overcome. First John 2:15-17 describes the things of this world as the cravings of sinful man, the lust of the eyes, and the boasting of what one has and does. Let's look at the foolishness of each of these.

- *The Cravings of Sinful Man.* This is characterized by a life lived for selfish pleasure. When we desire something, such as sexual relationship, emotional escape provided by drugs or alcohol, or satisfaction from food in large quantities, like a child we want it now! Quickly we alter our ethics, morality, and beliefs to get what we want when we want it. The world lives for pleasure with the motto "If it feels good, do it." But the transformed mind does not live this way. The transformed mind is sanctified by the Word of God. The transformed mind depends on God to have its needs fulfilled, and the transformed mind waits on Him.
- *The Lust of the Eyes.* Lust of the eyes doesn't have to do with sex but instead refers to the "need" to possess something. It could be a car, the latest shoes, a video game, or you name it! The world wants stuff to make it happy. For example, in

the popular video game "The Sims," we are comforted by
the purchase of material possessions. This game is actually
a reflection of what soothes us in life. The transformed
mind, however, does not focus on the temporal but on the
eternal. As a result, our desire is not for material wealth or
possessions but for the ability to leverage our resources to
advance the kingdom of God (see Matthew 6:19-21).

- *The Boasting of What We Have and Do.* Our status is
  important to us. Many people will live their entire life
  seeking to advance their position on earth. Especially for
  men, self-worth can be tied up in what we do more than
  in the person God made us to be. The transformed mind
  does not seek status in this world but seeks to leverage
  influence so that Christ may be made known. Jesus
  Himself did not seek the status of this world but rather
  made Himself a servant. We should seek to do likewise.

Many of the students described in this chapter could fall easily
into the trap of being worldly. Brandon could work to become a great
soccer player and live a lifestyle seeking status rather than serving
God. Clayton could easily seek fulfillment in only his video games
rather than finding it in God. Makenzie could go into acting, forsak-
ing her values and turning inward rather than serving mankind as
Christ did. The risk is there for all of these students to keep God
in a compartment or leave Him behind altogether. But video games,
soccer, and acting do not make one worldly; it is the mind we have as
we engage in these activities that defines us.

Others have gone before us and given guidance as to how to
integrate our faith. We'll call it *ambassadorship*.

THE AMBASSADOR CHRISTIAN

Second Corinthians 5:20 states, "We are therefore Christ's ambassadors, as though God were making his appeal through us." The Ambassador Christian realizes that God has given him a place in this world to represent the kingdom of heaven. In love, the Ambassador Christian seeks to advance the kingdom of God by allowing his life to be an example to those around him. Christian ambassadors view life through a different lens—one in which they do not represent themselves or the world. Instead, they openly represent Jesus Christ in all they do.

With this option in mind, let's examine the ways the students could integrate faith into their lives by using the Ambassador Christian model.

Brandon (soccer player) views his game and his relationships with teammates as a way to let his light shine. Through great sportsmanlike conduct and dedication to excellence, he can be a powerful witness to a life lived for Christ. When he is not able to attend youth group because of his game schedule, he asks his youth group to pray for his example. The youth group helps Brandon. They do fund-raising together, and they attend many of his games as youth group events so others can see the support the body of Christ has for one another. Brandon finds people, some his age and others older, to hold him accountable for good living in his life. They meet with him regularly and ask him tough questions about his life. One of his greatest challenges is being real with his teammates. Rather than try to appear as someone who has it all figured out (which none of us do in reality!), Brandon tries to be honest to teammates about his Christian life and ready to respond to any interest in it.

Makenzie (actress), like Brandon, sees her participation in dramatic productions as an opportunity to be salt and light where there is little. With the help of spiritually mature people, she develops a set of guidelines regarding what kind of roles and themes she is willing to participate in. Realizing that Hollywood rarely promotes strong Christian values, she knows that it may be difficult to find work and that locating a supportive local church is a top priority before making the move.

Clayton (Halo player) realizes that he loves games but loves people more. Games are just one meaningful way he can build healthy relationships with others. Clayton is selective about what game content he feels comfortable playing as a Christian. His video-game parties are a great way of introducing friends that would never darken the door of his church to Christian friends. He even has his youth pastor attend their game sessions so that his friends might feel more comfortable attending church events.

Jane (non-Christian family) realizes that the most important place to live for Christ is in her own home. She is sensitive to the fact that her parents are not familiar with the amazing truth of Jesus Christ and looks for ways to show them how much Jesus means to her. She makes a decision to serve her parents by honoring them, obeying them, and looking for ways to do things they haven't even asked her to do. A good day for Jane is when her parents say, "Wow, you are different!" and the greatest day will come when her folks want to know Jesus as their Savior.

J. T. (Christian school) decides to be a part of a program in an area he is interested in that does not involve being around church people. His hope is to be a light in a dark place rather than a candle in a well-lit room. Brandon also has decided to spend time learning about God on his own time rather than just swapping out his quiet time with his Bible schoolwork or chapel times. He is also challenging his friends to be genuine instead of hypocrites, even if that makes him unpopular. J. T. has trophies for Bible memory contests and can trump most in a game of Bible trivia, but he tries to remember that he still needs to be challenged by the Word of God and humbly listens to teaching from Scripture as if he has not heard it all before.

Chad (trapped by pornography) realizes that if he is struggling with this there are others who may be having the same temptations. In a bold move, Chad opens up to the guys in his youth group about his struggle, and his vulnerability inspires others to share their struggle. Together they form an accountability group to help each other be strong when they are weak.

Lauren ("good neighbor") decides to spend at least one hour a week visiting her sick neighbor. She is nervous at first but finds talking to her neighbor to be more rewarding than she would have thought. What's more, her sick (and dying) neighbor does not know about Jesus.

Josh (future doctor) decides that the road to a career in medicine will be challenging because so much of the scientific community is opposed to the idea of who God is. Josh also realizes that helping people in critical times of need will be just the right place for him to be an effective minister to others who do not know Christ. Josh wants to excel in his studies and career so he can have the platform to share Christ with others. Josh even considers giving a year or two of his time to serve as a medical missionary. He is excited about meeting the physical and medical needs of his patients as well as being able to help them spiritually.

Nicole (student) recognizes that her teacher clearly has more experience in argument and debate than she does. Knowing this, Nicole determines she must attempt to be the best student in the class if she is going to get the respect she needs from the teacher. She also realizes she will need to do additional study if she is going to be able to defend her position, so she seeks out resources and people who can help her grow in her ability to defend Christianity. Nicole has also determined that the classroom is not always the best place to challenge her teacher in a meaningful way; therefore, she develops a plan to engage the teacher in a more personal way throughout the semester.

For each situation, we've shown a way to integrate faith and living. While these solutions may be slightly oversimplified, they give us a vision of how we might learn to study, work, live, and play together in a manner that integrates what we believe about Christ into our everyday life. When we invite Christ out of the compartment we've kept Him in and give Him free rein in every aspect of our life, He will be there for us, everywhere we turn, challenging us and showing us how to be salt and light.

Think about what you've learned in this book, including the other practical applications of the mind: study and devotion, worship, solitude, evangelism, and apologetics. The big picture is simply integrating Christ so that He is in everything. If we do so, eventually our faith will pervade our lives until there is no longer a need for integration. Then, no matter what we study, what occupation we choose, or how we spend our free time, we will live a transformed life. Per Romans 12:1, our *entire* lives become a living sacrifice to the Lord, holy and pleasing to Him. This is our spiritual act of worship!

SMART THINKING

How would you describe your Christian life up to this point? Do you most resemble the Secluded Christian, Worldly Christian, or Ambassador Christian? You probably don't resemble all of one type. Most of us resemble each one at different times in our lives. For instance, at school you might seem more secluded, but in another group (such as a club) you might be more like an ambassador. Then, when you're out with friends on Friday night, by trying to fit in you might be the worldly Christian. Being consistent (the same in all walks of life) as an ambassador is your goal.

Using the paragraphs written about students in this chapter as an example, first write a paragraph describing a challenging aspect in your life now — a point at which there is tension between your life of faith and the parts of your life that shut out God. Then write a paragraph describing how this part of your life might look if you integrated your faith into that challenging area. (If you need help, ask your parents, pastor, and youth leader how they have integrated their faith into areas of their lives.)

Compare your paragraphs. Does the transformation seem possible? Will you bring your spiritual life into that aspect of your life that is missing integration? Ask God to show you how to do it and to help you cooperate with His agenda. Then trust Him to make the transformation His way.

WHERE TO THINK FROM HERE

We hope this book has inspired you to use your mind in more creative and effective ways. In our culture, informed thinking does not always come naturally, nor is it often encouraged. As you continue to mature in your Christian walk, you will always need to seek smart faith.

We've explored in this book how Christian thinking has become a lost and feared art (anti-intellectualism), what events in history made this possible, how our minds are structured and how to leverage that structure to transform them, what hinders us from developing smart faith, and how to apply smart faith to specific areas of our lives. That's some serious progress in and of itself!

Let this conclusion be a final encouragement to you.

BE A PART OF THE CHURCH TODAY

Regardless of your age, if you are a disciple of Christ, you are a member of the body of Christ. Your church needs you to do your part (even if you're too young to vote at business meetings yet) with the unique gifts and skills God has given you. Responsibilities in the church are not just for the adults; God also expects you to serve. You are part of the church of today (not tomorrow), and if you are going to do God's work, you need to jump in and get started. Will you help care for the spiritual needs of those younger than you? Will you join others in setting up for each service? Will you assist your Sunday school teacher? Will you take leadership in any way you can? If you don't know where or how you can serve, ask your youth leader or pastor or Sunday school teacher what you can do to help out. Don't take no for an answer.

SEEK THE WISDOM OF ELDERS

Don't be afraid of older people. Look beyond what you might consider old-fashioned to seek the wisdom people who have lived longer than you have gained. You can learn things two ways in this life: the easy way or the hard way. Christians who have lived longer have gathered much knowledge and wisdom by the experiences in their own lives and the lives of others. Find out what they know, and then take the wisdom and apply it to your life. Doing that will be much easier than learning through your own mistakes.

One reason we don't always use our minds well is that we spend time only with people our own age and rarely get introduced to ideas that have stood the test of time. Hanging out with only our group can mean we don't challenge one another and sometimes even reinforces wrong ideas.

LEARN ABOUT THE PAST

Learning about what has already happened and how the church got to the place it is today is essential in developing your Christian walk. See if you can find someone in your church who is interested in these things, too. Read biographies of great Christians who have gone before you—you'll likely find them inspiring.

SEEK OTHER THINKERS

It is often more fun to learn with others than in complete isolation, so find others in your church or community who really enjoy learning and seeking truth. If you can find a more mature Christian who enjoys stimulating thought, even better. I (Mark) am an introvert (that means I get energy from being alone), so I am not always inclined to seek others out. Yet I have found that if I do not, my spiritual life suffers and my mind begins to shut down. Likewise, extroverted people (they get energy from being with others) need to find times to be alone and reflect. Regardless, you need Christians who value intellectual development as part of discipleship in your life.

PASS THIS BOOK ALONG

To truly change the church and make God known, we need more Christians to understand how important their mind is to their spiritual development. You can pass this book along to a friend (buy them one, recommend it, give it away!) so that your entire generation can love God with the totality of their created being, including their mind.

NOTES

1. For more on the Puritans, see Allen Carden, *Puritan Christianity in America* (Grand Rapids, MI: Baker, 1990).
2. Carden, 186.
3. George Marsden, *Fundamentalism and American Culture* (New York: Oxford, 1980), 212.
4. For a critique of evolution, see Phillip E. Johnson, *Darwin on Trial*, 2d ed. (Downers Grove, IL: InterVarsity, 1993); also, J. P. Moreland, ed., *The Creation Hypothesis* (Downers Grove, IL: InterVarsity, 1994).
5. David Kinnamen, "Twentysomethings Struggle to Find Their Place in Christian Churches," *Barna Update*, September 24, 2003, www.barna.org.
6. Bruce Waltke states: "Since it (*galah*) is used of men as well as of God, it must not be thought of as a technical term for God's revelation. . . . Though not a technical term for divine revelation, the verb *galah* frequently conveys this meaning." See R. L. Harris, Gleason Archer, and Bruce Waltke, *Theological Wordbook of the Old Testament* (Chicago: Moody, 1988), 160.
7. For an excellent discussion of the nature of faith, see R. C. Sproul, John Gerstner, and Arthur Lindsley, *Classical Apologetics* (Grand Rapids, MI: Zondervan, 1984), 21, 191–196.
8. Jostein Gaarder, *Sophie's World: A Novel About the History of Philosophy*, trans. Paulette Moller (New York: Berkeley, 1997).
9. Technically, the problem is not that God is too big because God is not in space at all. Rather, God is too great to be the kind of being that could be spatial.
10. See J. P. Moreland, *Scaling the Secular City* (Grand Rapids, MI: Baker, 1986), chapter 3; Gary Habermas and J. P. Moreland, *Immortality: The Other Side of Death* (Nashville: Nelson, 1992),

chapters 1–3; J. P. Moreland, "A Defense of a Substance Dualist View of the Soul," in *Christian Perspectives on Being Human*, ed. J. P. Moreland and David M. Ciocchi (Grand Rapids, MI: Baker, 1993), 55–79.

11. 2002 Teens and Supernatural Report, conducted by Barna Research Group for WisdomWorks Ministries, Irving, TX (unpublished).

12. Martin E. P. Seligman, "Boomer Blues," *Psychology Today*, October 1988, 55.

13. See Christopher Lasch, *The Culture of Narcissism* (New York: Warner Books, 1979), especially chapter 2.

14. Jane M. Healy, *Endangered Minds: Why Children Don't Think and What We Can Do About It* (New York: Simon & Schuster, 1990), 114–116, 195–217.

15. Pitirim A. Sorokin, *The Crisis of Our Age* (Oxford: One World, 1941).

16. Sorokin.

17. Darrell Bock, *Breaking the Da Vinci Code: Answers to the Questions Everybody's Asking* (Nashville: Nelson, 2004).

18. Dan Brown, *The Da Vinci Code* (New York: Doubleday, 2003).

19. 2001 Teens and Evangelism Report, conducted by Barna Research Group for WisdomWorks Ministries, Irving, TX (unpublished).

20. E. Calvin Beisner, "A Reader's Guide to a Christian World View," *Discipleship Journal*, Issue 23, 1984, 37.

21. Martin Luther, *Table Talk*, cited in Richard Foster and James Smith, eds., *Devotional Classics* (San Francisco: Harper and Row, 1990), 132.

22. C. S. Lewis, *The Screwtape Letters* (New York: Macmillan, 1961), 20.

23. Aristotle's treatment of friendship is found in *Nichomachaen Ethics*, books 8 and 9. See also Paul J. Wadell, *Friendship and the Moral Life* (Notre Dame, IN: University of Notre Dame Press, 1989), especially chapters 2 and 3. See also Gilbert Meilaender, *Friendship: A Study in Theological Ethics* (Notre Dame, IN: University of Notre Dame Press, 1981).

ABOUT THE AUTHORS

J. P. Moreland is Distinguished Professor of philosophy at Talbot School of Theology, Biola University, and director of Eidos Christian Center. He is the author of numerous books and articles, including *Love Your God with All Your Mind* and *Philosophical Foundations for a Christian Worldview*.

Mark Matlock, president/founder of WisdomWorks Ministries and creator of planetwisdom.com, is the author of *Don't Buy the Lie* and *Freshman: The College Student's Guide to Developing Wisdom*. He is also a columnist for *Campus Life* magazine. Mark has spoken face-to-face with thousands of students, nationally and internationally, at his PlanetWisdom events. He resides in Irving, Texas, with his wife, Jade, and their two children, Dax and Skye.

OWN YOUR FAITH.